OCCASIONAL PAPER 207

Malaysia: From Crisis to Recovery

Kanitta Meesook, Il Houng Lee, Olin Liu, Yougesh Khatri,
Natalia Tamirisa, Michael Moore, and Mark H. Krysl

INTERNATIONAL MONETARY FUND
Washington DC
2001

© 2001 International Monetary Fund

Production: IMF Graphics Section
Figures: Theodore F. Peters, Jr.
Typesetting: Alicia Etchebarne-Bourdin

Cataloging-in-Publication Data

Malaysia: from crisis to recovery / Kanitta Meesook . . . [et al.]—Washington,
D.C.: International Monetary Fund, 2001.

   p. cm..—(Occasional paper, ISSN 0251-6365; no. 207)

    Includes bibliographical references.
    ISBN 1-58906-047-4

   1. Malaysia—Economic policy. 2. Malaysia—Economic conditions.
3. Fiscal policy—Malaysia. 4. Finance—Malaysia. I. Kanitta Meesook.
II. International Monetary Fund. III. Occasional paper (International Monetary Fund); no. 207

HC445.5.M36 2001

Price: US$20.00
(US$17.50 to full-time faculty members and
students at universities and colleges)

Please send orders to:
International Monetary Fund, Publication Services
700 19th Street, N.W., Washington, D.C. 20431, U.S.A.
Tel.: (202) 623-7430   Telefax: (202) 623-7201
E-mail: publications@imf.org
Internet: http://www.imf.org

recycled paper

Contents

The following symbols have been used throughout this paper:

. . .   to indicate that data are not available;

—   to indicate that the figure is zero or less than half the final digit shown, or that the item does not exist;

–   between years or months (e.g., 1998–99 or January–June) to indicate the years or months covered, including the beginning and ending years or months;

/   between years (e.g., 1998/99) to indicate a fiscal (financial) year.

"Billion" means a thousand million.

Minor discrepancies between constituent figures and totals are due to rounding.

The term "country," as used in this paper, does not in all cases refer to a territorial entity that is a state as understood by international law and practice; the term also covers some territorial entities that are not states, but for which statistical data are maintained and provided internationally on a separate and independent basis.

Preface

This occasional paper draws on staff background studies prepared for the 2000 and 2001 consultations between the International Monetary Fund and Malaysia. The paper takes stock of economic developments since the crisis and investigates various aspects of economic performance, policy, and reform that contributed to the strong recovery. The individual studies include the estimation of potential output and the implications for inflation; fiscal policy and key challenges for fiscal management; capital controls, their effects, and medium-term policy considerations; and performance and reform in the financial and corporate sectors.

The paper is the product of a team effort led by Kanitta Meesook. The team of authors comprised Il Houng Lee, Olin Liu, Yougesh Khatri, Natalia Tamirisa, Michael Moore, and Mark Krysl. Also central to the production of this paper was the research assistance of Janice Lee, and the coordination and assistance of Margaret Tan and Lisa Vassou.

The authors would like to thank the Malaysian authorities for their excellent cooperation and support during policy discussions and technical meetings, and for the extensive provision of data and background materials. The authors would also like to thank—without implication—Kalpana Kochhar for reviewing drafts of the entire paper at an early stage, Mark O'Brien for reviewing Section VI, and Jenifer Piesse for contributing to the empirical work in Section VII. The authors are also indebted to the External Relations Department and to Gail Berre who edited the paper and coordinated its production and publication.

The opinions expressed are solely those of the authors and do not necessarily reflect the views of the International Monetary Fund, the Executive Directors, or the Malaysian authorities.

Except where otherwise indicated, the paper reflects information available through end-2000.

I Overview

Olin Liu

As an emerging market economy, Malaysia is clearly a success story. During the past three decades, the Malaysian government has implemented a number of medium- to long-term development plans, starting with the 20-year New Economic Policy—a development plan that strived for greater economic well-being for the ethnic Malays, or *bumiputras*—and followed by the National Development Policy in the early 1990s. More recently, the Third Outline Perspective Plan provides the general thrust of Malaysia's development strategy for the period 2001–10.

Malaysia's development plans were implemented effectively. From 1970 to the mid-1990s, the country's investment ratio was among the highest in the region, resulting in a dramatic shift in the structure of the economy from agriculture and mining to a growing reliance on manufacturing. Liberalization measures were introduced across the board that helped improve competitiveness and productivity. Much of the investment went into electronics and other export-oriented industries, while a large portion also went into nontradable sectors including capital-intensive infrastructure and the real estate sector.

The development plans were initially financed by public funds. As a result, by the early 1980s, growth was accompanied by increased budget deficits and an unsustainable level of public debt. The authorities took measures to reduce the government deficit, and successfully restored fiscal prudence. Structural adjustments were also undertaken, including an open trade and payments system that helped expand rapidly Malaysia's export base. Sustained high growth during the 1980s brought significant improvements in living standards and social cohesion. Economic diversification, coupled with deregulation and liberalization of the financial system, also helped transform the country into a middle-income emerging market by the end of that decade.

Malaysia's strong economic performance continued during the 1990s prior to the crisis. Real output growth averaged 8½ percent a year; unemployment was below 3 percent; prices and the exchange rate remained stable; and international reserves were robust. However, there were also signs of stress as exports decelerated and a large current account deficit developed in the context of a gradual appreciation of the effective exchange rate. While the investment-led growth strategy was successful in raising output and income, investment quality had deteriorated. This eventually led to major balance sheet weaknesses in the banking and corporate sectors, exposing the economy to the contagion of the Asian crisis. Similar to its neighbors, Malaysia went through a currency crisis and a banking crisis, but its low level of external debt spared it from an external debt crisis.

Malaysia's economic vulnerabilities stepped up significantly from early 1997 through the period following the onset of the crisis in mid-1997, as market confidence increasingly diminished along with the rest of the region. Large portfolio outflows took place, and equity and property values declined substantially. The ringgit came under tremendous pressure. As currency traders took speculative positions in the offshore ringgit market in anticipation of a large devaluation, the offshore ringgit interest rates increased markedly relative to domestic rates. This heightened upward pressure on domestic interest rates, intensified outflows of ringgit funds, and exacerbated banks' liquidity problems and overall financial distress. The Malaysian corporate sector experienced significant loss of wealth as a result of sharp falls in the value of real estate and equities used as bank collateral. Corporate incomes and cash flows also declined, leaving some corporations unable to service their debt.

The initial response of the authorities was to hike interest rates and tighten fiscal policy in an attempt to anchor market confidence in the financial system. In early 1998, fiscal policy was revised to a more expansionary stance. This policy mix proved to be insufficient to correct external imbalances and bring about the needed economic adjustment. The contagion effects of the crisis and the associated economic contraction were far worse than anticipated. Domestic imbalances quickly emerged as growth rates slowed and then turned sharply negative in early 1998. Market confidence faltered amid adverse regional developments and uncertainties. Anticipation of further devaluation of the ringgit heightened. By the summer of 1998, the stock market had fallen to its lowest level in recent history.

In September 1998, the Malaysian authorities launched a policy package designed to insulate monetary policy from external volatility. Measures included an exchange rate pegged to the U.S. dollar and selected exchange and capital controls, complemented by a fiscal stimulus package that stepped up capital spending. These measures permitted the subsequent lowering of interest rates. The authorities also pursued fundamental reforms in the financial and corporate sectors, including a bank consolidation program and an upgrading of prudential regulation and supervision in line with international best practices.

Malaysia's recovery in 1999–2000 was among the strongest of the Asian crisis economies, led by buoyant world demand for electronics and supported by accommodating macroeconomic policies. The external current account turned into large surpluses, allowing a buildup of international reserves. Unemployment declined, and inflation remained low. The strong growth and a gradual easing of capital controls helped improve investor confidence. The recovery was also accompanied by reduced vulnerability of the financial system. Although operational restructuring of the corporate sector has been somewhat slow, much progress was achieved with corporate debt restructuring.

Since the latter part of 2000, however, downside risks for Malaysia have increased. Heavy dependence on electronic exports made Malaysia highly sensitive to the global slowdown in information technology. Sharp depreciations of the yen and other regional currencies have resulted in a large effective appreciation of the ringgit, particularly during late March and early April 2001, leading in turn to short-term capital outflows and reserve losses. These developments, at a time when the economy was already being hit hard by the global slowdown, has adversely affected market confidence. Nevertheless, Malaysia's external vulnerability is relatively well contained: the current account continues to maintain a large surplus; short-term external debt is low; and reserves have remained adequate. Progress in financial sector restructuring has also improved the capacity of banks to manage risks.

Looking ahead, the issue is how Malaysia can better protect itself from future shocks and avoid another crisis while it seeks to regain its position as one of the fastest growing economies in the world. To these ends, its strategy should include continued structural reforms to achieve healthy balance sheets of the banking and corporate sectors; further deregulation to promote competition and efficiency; and consistent macroeconomic policies to maintain financial stability and sustainable fiscal and external positions.

The sections that follow review policy issues and aspects of economic management that have been associated with Malaysia's progress from a major crisis to a strong recovery, and their implications for the future. Section II presents a comparative review of the country's policies and performance during 1997–2000; Section III describes the study and estimation of potential output and inflation dynamics; Section IV reviews fiscal policy management; Section V discusses the capital controls introduced in September 1998 and their impact; Section VI summarizes various aspects of financial sector restructuring; and Section VII reviews developments in corporate sector reforms.

II Comparative Review of Policies and Performance, 1997–2000

Kanitta Meesook

Malaysia has received much attention since September 1998 when, in response to a deteriorating economic situation emanating from the Asian crisis, it introduced capital and exchange controls. Also, Prime Minister Mahathir Mohamad rebuked policy advice from the IMF that Malaysia had followed up to then.[1] Initially there was concern that these controls might be used to avoid needed policy adjustment, and investors and market analysts reacted negatively. Market assessment turned more positive, however, as it became clear that Malaysia's macroeconomic policies were not out of line, that the undervalued pegged exchange rate was contributing to the rapid recovery of exports and output, and that financial sector reforms were being vigorously pursued.

This section reviews the developments from the emergence of the Asian crisis to end-2000, comparing Malaysia's initial conditions, policy responses, and recent performance with those of the other crisis countries.

Initial Conditions and Economic Structure

Malaysia's economic structure and performance were relatively strong prior to the crisis (see Appendix Figure A.2.1). Real GDP grew rapidly, while inflation was low. At the same time, fiscal policy was prudent, domestic savings were high, international reserves were robust, and external debt was well managed. The legal and regulatory frameworks were also comparatively well developed.

Underlying these positive features, however, were signs of overheating and structural vulnerability, broadly similar to the other crisis countries (Appendix Figure A.2.2). A predictably stable exchange rate encouraged foreign borrowing and dis-

couraged the use of hedging instruments. From the early 1990s, this allowed large current account deficits—brought about in part by the appreciation of the real effective exchange rate (Figure 2.1)—to be sustained by short-term capital inflows, including through the stock market. Rapid credit growth led to excessive investment and resource misallocation, fueling asset price bubbles in property and stock markets. As the financial system and capital markets were liberalized, the important aspects of supervision and regulation remained weak, allowing extensive connected lending and obscuring the true scale of financial and corporate problems. Furthermore, an active—but largely unregulated—offshore market for the ringgit exposed the currency market to information asymmetries and excessive risk taking by private investors. All these elements contributed to Malaysia's susceptibility to contagion by the crisis.

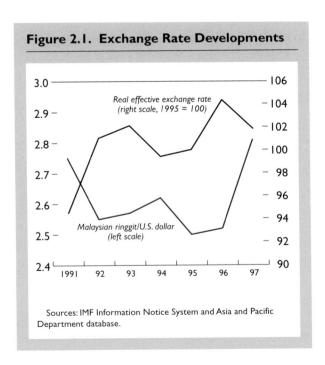

Figure 2.1. Exchange Rate Developments

Real effective exchange rate (right scale, 1995 = 100)

Malaysian ringgit/U.S. dollar (left scale)

Sources: IMF Information Notice System and Asia and Pacific Department database.

---

[1]Deputy Prime Minister and Minister of Finance, Anwar Ibrahim, was Malaysia's key contact with the IMF at that time. He was removed from office the day after the capital and exchange controls were introduced.

After Thailand was forced to float the baht in July 1997, Malaysia's exchange and stock markets came under severe pressure. Large capital outflows that had started in April that year continued, inducing a rapid adjustment in the current account and a significant depreciation of the ringgit along with other regional currencies (Appendix Figure A.2.3). Arbitrage between domestic and offshore ringgit markets became more active; in anticipation of further weakening of the currency, the premium on offshore ringgit interest rates increased sharply, exacerbating outflows of ringgit funds and the domestic liquidity shortage.

Moreover, domestic demand collapsed because of negative wealth effects from falling equity and property prices and uncertain economic prospects (Appendix Figure A.2.4). External demand also declined, consistent with financial difficulties and falling demand in other crisis countries. As a result of the ringgit's depreciation, higher borrowing costs, declines in equity price, and the drop in demand, corporate balance sheets deteriorated further. Thus, the financial system came under increasing stress (Figure 2.2), reflecting in part high corporate leverage, and signs of bank runs emerged in late 1997. As the market recognized that the asset quality of both the banks and corporations was worse than it appeared, confidence eroded further.

Malaysia's relative strengths going into the crisis nonetheless helped contain the severity of its impact. Although Malaysia suffered serious currency and financial crises, it was spared from an external debt crisis. Thus, unlike the other countries, Malaysia did not require a large official financing package or debt rescheduling.[2] In addition to overall financial prudence, the credibility of the financial system benefited from a widespread bank restructuring undertaken in the 1980s. These strong features protected the country's external position and may have lessened the extent of the overall output decline. The magnitude of domestic unemployment and potential social disruption was moderated further by a significant migrant workforce that acted as a buffer.

Capital Account Regime and Reserve Management

Malaysia's initial low level of short-term external debt enabled it to maintain foreign reserves at a reasonably high level, and this contributed to relatively robust external and domestic confidence early on in the crisis. As a consequence of financial vigilance exercised through prudential regulation of capital movements,[3] the exposure of the financial and corporate systems was contained. Management of foreign exchange reserves has been cautious, entailing no forward sales or other off-balance-sheet liabilities, so that all reserves have been usable.

The capital account was nevertheless liberal in ways that left Malaysia vulnerable to contagion. Like the other countries, portfolio flows were free of restrictions; in Malaysia, these were the main channel for capital outflows in mid- and late 1997. Furthermore, cross-border activities in ringgit were treated liberally, permitting the use of the currency in trade and financial transactions with nonresidents, and in offshore trading of securities listed on local exchanges. As a consequence, an offshore ringgit market developed and became more active than those in other affected countries.

Openness and Structure of Exports

Malaysia is the most open among the crisis countries (Table 2.1), and this feature was beneficial in leading output recovery in early 1999 even as domestic demand remained relatively weak. However, the country's export base has become more dependent on electronic and electrical products, whose share in total exports reached more than 60 percent that year. Thus, like the other countries, Malaysia could become more vulnerable to adverse world de-

Figure 2.2. Bank Lending

Nonperforming loans of the banking system (in percent of total loans)

Credit to private sector (four-quarter percent change)

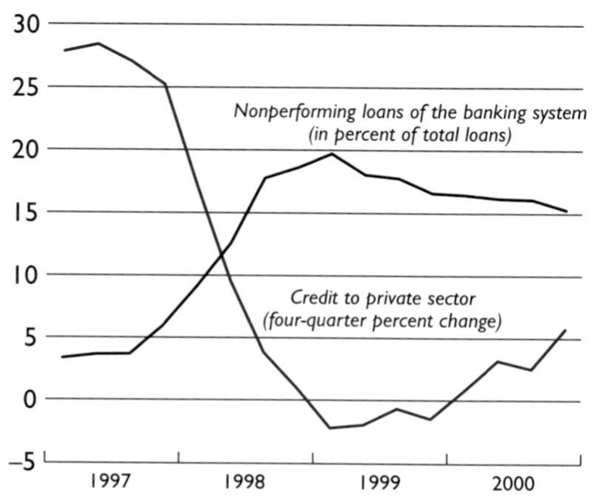

Source: CEIC Data Company Limited.

---

[2]Malaysia was the only one of the five Asian countries severely affected by the crisis that did not resort to use of IMF resources.

[3]Such regulation included limits on banks' net foreign currency open position and monitoring of liabilities of domestic corporations to ensure their foreign exchange earning potential.

Table 2.1. Asian Crisis Countries: Selected Structural Indicators, 1996–2000

(In percent, unless otherwise indicated)

	Malaysia	Korea	Thailand	Philippines	Indonesia
External					
Precrisis					
Openness, sum of exports and imports as percent of GDP, 1996	148	54	69	63	42
Share of exports to Japan and other crisis countries, 1996	23	21	25	27	38
Export growth in U.S. dollars, second half of 1995–second half of 1996	1	–3	–5	16	6
Postcrisis					
Openness, sum of exports and imports as percent of GDP, 2000	186	70	93	98	64
Share of exports to Japan and other crisis countries, second half of 1999–first half of 2000	22	19	23	24	34
Export growth in U.S. dollars, 1999–2000	13	22	11	15	19
Banking system					
Precrisis					
Nonperforming loans as share of total loans, end-1997[1]	6	6	23	5	7
Credit to private sector annual growth, average of 1993–96	21	20	31	40	22
Credit to private sector, in percent of GDP, 1996	141	150	135	52	59
Loan-to-deposit ratio (M2-based), end-1997	1.0	1.6	1.4	1.0	1.2
Postcrisis					
Nonperforming loans as share of total loans, end-2000[1,2]	15	7	18	15	26
Impaired assets as shares of interest-earning assets, end-2000[3]	22	23	38	23	61
Credit to private sector annual growth, 2000[4]	6	–2	1	8	17
Credit to private sector, in percent of GDP, 2000[4]	139	133	125	46	23
Loan-to-deposit ratio (M2-based), end-2000[5]	0.9	1.2	0.9	0.7	0.4
Corporate sector					
Precrisis					
Corporate debt/equity ratios, 1997[6]	88	425	440	174	334
Market capitalization in percent of GDP, 1996	317	28	56	98	41
Stock price changes, 1990–96	145	–6	36	385	53
Postcrisis					
Corporate debt/equity ratios, 2000[6]	114	235	280	186	277
Market capitalization in percent of GDP, 2000	131	35	26	79	21
Stock price changes, mid-1997–end-2000	–37	–32	–49	–47	–43

Sources: IMF, *International Financial Statistics*; *World Economic Outlook*; IMF staff estimates and CEIC database.

[1]Definitions of nonperforming loans vary among different countries, and caution should be applied in making any comparison.

[2]Data cover only loans that remain in the banking system, that is, not including nonperforming loans transferred to asset management agencies. Korea refers to end-September.

[3]Data include nonperforming loans transferred to asset management agencies.

[4]Unadjusted for transfers of nonperforming loans to asset management agencies. Thailand data refer to end-October.

[5]Korea and Philippines refer to end-November, and Indonesia refers to end-August.

[6]Nonfinancial companies. Malaysia, Thailand, and Indonesia are listed companies only.

velopments in the period ahead, especially in regard to the technology sector.

Investment-Based Growth Strategy

For two decades prior to the crisis, Malaysia pursued a policy strategy aimed at raising economic growth and eradicating poverty by promoting investment in priority sectors and equipping the *bumiputras* with capital and opportunities to engage in various economic activities. For a number of years, the investment ratio for Malaysia was the highest among the crisis countries (Figure 2.3). This strategy was successful in generating one of the highest precrisis growth rates and elevating the income and wealth of the *bumiputras*.

Although much of the investment went into electronics and other export-oriented industries, a large portion went into capital-intensive infrastructure and the real estate sector. Investment quality, measured by the incremental capital output ratio and estimated total factor productivity growth, eroded significantly

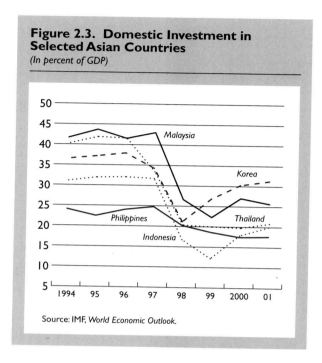

Figure 2.3. Domestic Investment in Selected Asian Countries
(In percent of GDP)

Source: IMF, *World Economic Outlook.*

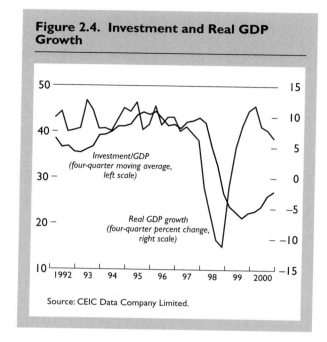

Figure 2.4. Investment and Real GDP Growth

Source: CEIC Data Company Limited.

between 1990–97.[4] As the Malaysian economy underwent an adjustment in response to the crisis, private investment declined sharply in 1998 and has remained subdued (Figure 2.4). This adjustment dampened short-term domestic demand during the recovery process, but reallocation from overinvested sectors would be desirable to improve the investment efficiency and achieve higher total factor productivity growth over the long term. In this connection, the planned move to a knowledge-based economy (K-economy) is intended both to raise the productivity of investment and to diversify exports, although its effects will not be immediate.

Capital Market Development

Beginning in the early 1980s, a rapidly growing capital market emerged as a major funding source for higher investment (Figure 2.5). Its development was supported by a number of measures to strengthen, broaden, and deepen the market, which improved the regulatory framework, as well as the trading and settlement infrastructure.

Stock market capitalization in Malaysia grew to an extremely high level prior to the crisis, reflecting both the fast expansion of the capital market and liberal capital account regime. At the same time, the level of corporate bank (short-term) indebtedness was among the highest of the crisis countries (Figure 2.6). As the crisis emerged, sharp declines in the stock market led to relatively greater losses of wealth in Malaysia than in other countries. This had negative implications for corporate ability to roll over or service debt, because the value of stockholdings used as bank collateral fell abruptly and income streams from them diminished. Multiple leveraging—made possible by cross-holding structures—exacerbated the negative impact on corporate wealth and cash flows, and consequently on the extent of financial distress. This may explain, in part, the relative worsening of Malaysia's corporate performance in 1997–98. Low rates of return on capital, stemming from overinvestment in the past, have likely contributed as well.

Legal and Regulatory Framework

Malaysia's well-developed legal and regulatory frameworks, which provided reasonable protection to creditors and noncontrolling shareholders, permitted relatively speedy but orderly settlement of problem loans early on. Furthermore, priority had been given to strengthening and modernizing prudential safeguards even before the crisis. This, compared with the weaker systems (including the absence of

---

[4]For total factor productivity growth estimates, see Michael Meow-Chung Yap, 2000, "Potential Output of the Malaysian Economy: Evaluating the Production Function Approach," paper presented at the Malaysian Institute of Economic Research, November (Kuala Lumpur). The incremental capital output ratio reversed in 1998–99, which was attributed largely to falling investment.

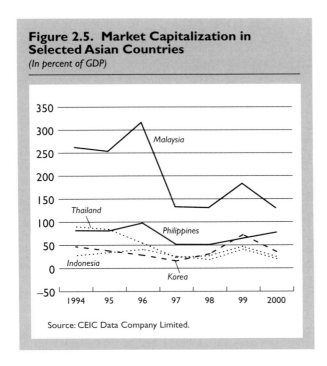

Figure 2.5. Market Capitalization in Selected Asian Countries
(In percent of GDP)

Source: CEIC Data Company Limited.

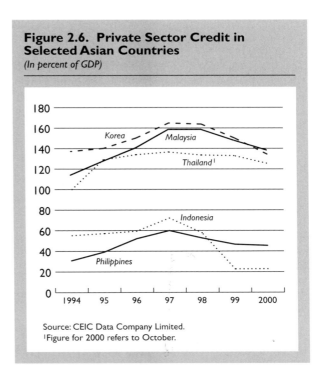

Figure 2.6. Private Sector Credit in Selected Asian Countries
(In percent of GDP)

Source: CEIC Data Company Limited.
[1]Figure for 2000 refers to October.

enforceable bankruptcy laws) and lack of supervisory personnel in some other countries, helped maintain confidence in and facilitate the recovery process of Malaysia's economy.

Still, as in the other countries, close connections between large corporations and the Malaysian government masked the extent of deterioration in the asset quality of financial and corporate systems before the crisis, and this situation appears to have continued even after the crisis. Implicit government guarantees associated with privatized infrastructure projects undertaken prior to 1998 may have deferred debt and operational restructuring by the concerned corporations even as they became financially illiquid. The government also influenced bank lending to certain projects that it deemed of social importance. These practices could have potentially adverse implications for future claims on the government.[5]

Social and Political Cohesion

The *bumiputra* policy, the presence of temporary migrant workers, and smooth relations between labor unions and employers help explain the low unemployment in Malaysia even at the depth of the crisis. Cost reductions in sectors facing output contraction were brought about through nonrenewal of contracts for migrant workers. However, as far as domestic labor was concerned, retrenchment was limited, as employers implemented other practices (also used in other crisis countries), such as part-time, flexi-time, and pay cuts, before resorting to layoffs. These "labor hoarding" practices were reversed as the economy recovered. Importantly, progress in poverty reduction over the past two decades has helped preserve overall social and political stability.

Policy Responses and Performance

The capital controls and the ringgit peg introduced in September 1998 were key policy measures that distinguished Malaysia from the rest of the crisis countries.[6] At that time, it was difficult to tell whether financial instability in the region was likely to intensify or abate. Some measure of stability had by then begun to return to the regional financial markets (Appendix Figure A.2.5). From late August 1998, local currencies and stock markets had broadly calmed down, and forward exchange rate forecasts showed expectations that the ringgit—as well as the won and the baht—would stabilize. Short-term interest rates had declined to levels below 10 percent. Sovereign bond spreads had peaked for Thailand, Korea, and the Philippines. In

---

[5]See Section III for further discussions of fiscal issues.

[6]See, below, the time frame of Malaysia's policies in response to the crisis and economic performance that ensued.

both Thailand and Malaysia, the offshore swap differential was trending down; nevertheless, the differential was in a high range and financial market pressures also remained high.

Given the relative stability experienced by the region, Malaysia's approach seems to have made little difference to the monetary policy outcomes or structural reforms. Crisis countries that did not introduce these measures have been just as able to carry out accommodating monetary policy and maintain stable exchange rates. Boosted by rising export demand for electronic goods, especially from the United States, economic recovery has been broadly similar across the Asian crisis countries (Appendix Figure A.2.6). Malaysia entered the crisis later, however, and the resumption of domestic demand also came later. All countries embarked on structural reforms, but Malaysia's progress in financial restructuring with active involvement of the government has been more rapid. Malaysia's prudential regulation and supervision, already reasonably well developed prior to the crisis, also seems to be superior, contributing to a relatively robust financial system that could help cushion Malaysia's vulnerability against future crises.

The imposition of capital controls led to higher costs of external borrowing for Malaysia, but only temporarily. Bolstered by the pegged exchange rate at an undervalued level, the controls provided a safeguard to policymakers and domestic market participants at a time of financial volatility. Overall, the adverse impact of capital control measures was contained (Appendix Figure A.2.7).[7]

Fiscal and Monetary Policies

Macroeconomic policy responses were broadly similar in all the crisis countries. Sharp hikes in interest rates and fiscal tightening aimed at restoring confidence were implemented initially. As the severity of output declines became evident, the strategy shifted to fiscal expansion supported by accommodating monetary policies. The magnitude, timing, and degree of flexibility of policy responses in Malaysia, however, were different from the other countries to some extent. Later implementation of macroeconomic stimuli, consistent with the delayed output weakening and combined with rigidities in both the budget system and interest rate structure, may have led to relatively slow responses in domestic demand. In 2000–01, Malaysia continued to pursue fiscal expansion, whereas the other countries had moved to a more neutral stance (Appendix Figure A.2.8).

There were also delays in implementing fiscal stimulus measures in Malaysia. Fiscal restraint was pursued at the early stage of the crisis, consistent with the policy recommendations of the IMF. Once fiscal expansion was adopted, the delays arose from reliance on increased capital expenditures, which produced slower effects than higher current spending or the tax cuts applied in some other countries. This approach in turn reflects the policy of maintaining an operating surplus each year. The impact on private domestic demand of the 1998–99 fiscal impulse—estimated to be the largest among the crisis countries—was not fully felt until late 1999, reflecting the lags in carrying out capital spending. This may explain the lag in the recovery. Fiscal analysis is complicated, however, by the use of off-budget privatized infrastructure projects to stimulate the economy, the magnitude of which is not transparent.

In the early stage of the crisis, Malaysia did not defend domestic currency as aggressively as the other countries. Nominal and real interest rates were raised, but reached lower peaks in Malaysia, and very high interest rates (reaching 35 percent) persisted for only a few days. The situation contrasted with those in Korea and Thailand, where high interest rates were maintained for some months without interruption. The difference reflects two factors inherent in the initial conditions of the three countries. First, Malaysia's financing gap, if any, was modest, and the maintenance of high interest rates to attract capital inflows was less critical. Second, the Malaysian corporate sector relied more on domestic borrowing than external borrowing; therefore, Malaysia's strategy helped mitigate the impact of the crisis on the sector's financial distress, whereas the strategy used in the other countries helped in the stabilization of the exchange rates that was needed to contain external debt-service burden.

As monetary policy eased, real interest rates in Malaysia were brought down to a level slightly lower than in the other crisis countries (Appendix Figure A.2.9), but the interest rate structure in Malaysia remained rigid (as in Thailand). Slow credit growth was observed in all countries and does not appear to have constrained the recovery because demand for large investments was small. Interest rate rigidities, in particular, ceilings on banks' lending rates, could have nevertheless hindered productive—but higher risk—activities and prevented faster output growth.

To counter the slow credit extension, Malaysia set nonbinding, minimum targets for loan growth, gave tax incentives, and made use of directed lending to target specific sectors. In the environment of subdued domestic demand and excess liquidity that prevailed through 2000, these measures appeared ineffective. Government involvement in negotiations to restructure bank debt of some privatized infrastruc-

---

[7]See Section V for further discussions of the capital controls and their impact.

ture projects, for example through the Corporate Debt Restructuring Committee, may have boosted credit extension, although it could also have implications for future claims on the government.

Capital Controls and Exchange Rate Regime

The effect of the September 1998 controls in curtailing speculative capital outflows appeared benign because much of this capital had already left Malaysia (Figure 2.7). Crisis countries that did not adopt capital controls were able to pursue a low interest rate policy and to keep exchange rates relatively stable as the surplus from the current account began to build up and capital outflows subsided. These countries also made some progress with financial and corporate sector restructuring. Nevertheless, the policies provided safety measures at a time of foreign exchange market instability. Domestic market participants reacted positively to the fixed exchange rate regime, although it had exposed them to exchange risks by discouraging hedging activities. The effects of control measures on raising funding costs for Malaysia and limiting capital inflows were reversed soon after the controls were eased.

The magnitude of the ringgit undervaluation appears to have been roughly similar to those of the other currencies. The undervalued ringgit benefited the Malaysian export sector, but it may have also discouraged imports and associated investment in other sectors and contributed to the slow pickup in private investment overall. Additionally, market expectations of an appreciation, which prevailed from early 1999 to mid-2000, are likely to have induced short-term speculative inflows that were subsequently followed by outflows and reserve losses.

Financial Sector Reforms

Policy responses to strengthen the financial system have also been broadly similar among the crisis countries. To prevent its collapse, all countries gave a blanket deposit guarantee and provided liquidity support early into the crisis. Subsequently, each country established some form of asset-management strategy to address nonperforming loan problems, gave high priority to the upgrading of supervisory and regulatory standards to international best practices, and sought to recapitalize their financial institutions based on those norms. In the process, bank closures or merger programs were undertaken to establish stronger financial systems.

Overall, the progress achieved by Malaysia and Korea compares favorably in some aspects to the other countries, contributing to the improved perfor-

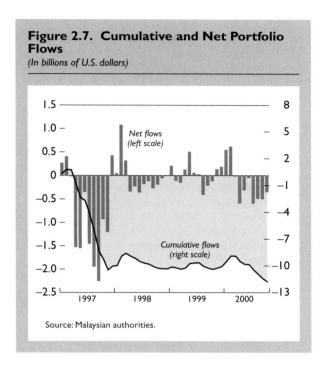

Figure 2.7. Cumulative and Net Portfolio Flows
(In billions of U.S. dollars)

Source: Malaysian authorities.

mance of the financial systems.[8] This may be explained to some extent by the more centralized approach they adopted that permitted actions to be taken early and in a comprehensive manner, and, in the case of Malaysia, by its better starting conditions as well. A more active involvement by the government, however, implies that it could be taking higher risks on contingent liabilities involved in the restructuring process and on implicit guarantees of the future health of the financial system and of corporations affected by these actions. Risks would diminish, to the extent that ongoing reforms of the regulatory and supervisory frameworks promote greater market discipline and better-managed financial institutions. The various aspects of Malaysia's financial and corporate sector reforms can be summarized as follows:

- The government announced a guarantee of bank deposits early in the crisis (January 1998) that was credible in view of the country's legal and regulatory framework, and the country did not suffer the bank runs experienced in Indonesia, Korea, and Thailand.

- Danamodal, the recapitalization agency, succeeded early in restoring the capital levels of domestic banks in Malaysia, whereas the capital standards had not fully been met in some of the other crisis countries that employed a more de-

---

[8]See Section VI for more details on financial sector developments and reform measures.

centralized process. The agency's mandate inspired confidence that all domestic financial institutions in Malaysia would be recapitalized to the required standards and that necessary operational restructuring would be imposed through the exercise of control over their managements.

- The special legal power vested in Danaharta, the centralized asset management company, helped ensure that banks were left with a manageable level of problem loans and that acquired assets were rehabilitated; this contrasts with the more decentralized nonperforming loan workout in Thailand. The use of independent auditors to determine the value of assets acquired by Danaharta avoided the subsidies required in Indonesia and in Korea. The emphasis placed on the management of assets implies their disposal at a more measured pace, unlike the quick disposal of acquired assets by Danaharta's counterparts in other crisis countries. The agency succeeded in the early closure of its window for acquiring nonperforming loans and achieved a relatively high recovery rate of disposed loans, but the risk of its becoming a nonperforming loan warehouse is greater under the current strategy unless assets are upgraded and sold before long.

- The bank consolidation program, tightly coordinated by Bank Negara Malaysia, aimed at creating larger and more efficient financial institutions ready to compete globally as new foreign competition is allowed. This contrasts with the strategy elsewhere, which entails bank closures and takeovers of existing banks—including by foreign investors—thereby imposing market discipline and requiring financial institutions to become internationally competitive rapidly.[9] Malaysia's approach has been less disruptive, but the government's reluctance to close banks could create moral hazard. Limited foreign equity participation in local banks could also slow the diffusion of technology transfers and the adoption of international best practices.

- Malaysia moved ahead of the other crisis countries to strengthen prudential supervision and regulation. Bank Negara Malaysia's move toward internal risk management by banks, including for cross-border transactions, and toward risk-based and consolidated supervision is a major step to enhance the soundness of the financial system, especially if financial innovations are to be increasingly embraced by the country's banking system.

Corporate Reforms

Progress in corporate sector reforms in Malaysia has been mixed.[10] Institutional frameworks have been upgraded, especially standards for corporate governance. The promotion of active bond markets is expected to help gradually rebalance the maturity profile of corporate debt and diversify system risks. However, like in the other crisis countries, improved corporate balance sheets have largely been a result of economic recovery and debt restructuring, whereas progress in operational restructuring has been slow. Furthermore, a few incidents of poor governance despite the upgraded standards have raised doubts about the government's commitment to adhere to best practices and protect minority shareholders. Such incidents have in turn undermined confidence and stock market performance, and weakened the ability of corporations to raise equity to support the restructuring process.

Time Frame of Malaysia's Response to the Crisis

Initial Policy Response

From the time the Thai baht was floated in July 1997 until February 1998, Malaysia's policies (Table 2.2) broadly aimed at addressing external imbalances, alleviating pressures on the ringgit, and restoring market confidence. For a few days in July 1997, the authorities intervened in the exchange market and raised interbank interest rates sharply, but they quickly let the ringgit depreciate and lowered the interest rate to near precrisis levels. In August 1997, administrative measures were introduced to regulate foreign exchange swap transactions[11] and restrict trading of blue chip stocks in the Kuala Lumpur stock exchange.

As output expansion continued to be brisk through end-1997, macroeconomic policies during this period showed considerable restraint. Fiscal policy was tightened through sharp spending cuts. Steps were introduced to reduce loan growth through lending targets and directives to banks to cut credit for

---

[9]The share of foreign-owned banks in Malaysia was relatively high before the crisis, although their activities are more restricted than local banks. The approach to not allow foreign takeovers of banks may partly explain the low level of foreign direct investment flows into the country in 1998–2000, relative to recent history, in comparison with such flows into the other crisis countries.

[10]See Section VII for further analysis of the corporate sector and recent reform efforts.

[11]In May 1997, Thailand imposed partial restrictions on offshore activities in order to stabilize the foreign exchange market and stem speculative attacks on the baht.

Table 2.2. Major Economic Policy Measures During Emergence of Crisis and Early Stage of Contagion

Date/Background	Policy Objectives	Specific Measures
March 1997: Kuala Lumpur stock exchange price began to fall	Monetary: To slow credit growth	• Limits on lending to the real estate sector and for the purchase of stocks and shares
July 1997: Thai baht devalued	Monetary: To defend the ringgit	• Interbank rate raised, reaching 35 percent for a couple of weeks, then lowered to around 10 percent
August 1997: Ringgit depreciation continued; Thailand's program with IMF	Monetary: To limit interest rate hikes and break links between domestic and offshore rates	• Bank Negara Malaysia abandoned ringgit defense • Limits imposed on ringgit swap transactions with nonresidents that were non trade related
	Stock market: To stabilize and support Kuala Lumpur stock exchange price	• Ban introduced on trading of blue-chip stocks comprising Kuala Lumpur stock exchange composite index • Announcement of a large, publicly funded stock support scheme
September 1997: Prime minister's statement that currency trading should be illegal	Fiscal: To strengthen fiscal and external accounts	• Government spending cut for 1997, and implementation of large privatized projects deferred
October 1997: Indonesia's program with IMF	Fiscal: To continue cautious plan	• 1998 budget announced, targeting a surplus of 2½ percent of GDP (corresponding to a real growth rate of 7 percent)
	Monetary: To limit credit growth	• Credit plan introduced to limit loan growth gradually to 15 percent by end-1998, but with loans to specified sectors encouraged • Base lending rates allowed to rise in response to higher interbank rates
November 1997: Further fall in stock prices	Corporate: To rescue Renong which was in financial trouble	• Proposed takeover of Renong by United Engineers Malaysia announced
December 1997: Evidence of slowing activity; Korea's program with IMF	Fiscal: To maintain broad fiscal target for 1998	• Major cuts (18 percent) in government spending plan for 1998, offsetting lower revenue projections and corresponding to revised output growth of 4–5 percent
	Monetary: To support the ringgit	• Bank Negara Malaysia intervened in foreign exchange interbank market
January 1998: Signs of bank runs and flight to quality	Financial: To provide stability	• National Economic Action Council set up as consultative body to deal with the Asian crisis • Government announced a guarantee of deposits at all financial institutions • Tighter restrictions imposed on stockbroking companies including those on gearing ratios, margin financing, and total exposure
February 1998	Corporate: To strengthen corporate governance	• High Level Finance Committee on Corporate Governance established
	Monetary: To rebalance macropolicy	• Bank Negara Malaysia intervention rate raised to 11 percent from 10 percent; statutory reserve requirement cut to 10 percent from 13½ percent • Bank Negara Malaysia set guidelines to ensure credit to priority bumiputra, housing, and small business sectors • Announcement that five financial institutions were in need of recapitalization, but no specific plans provided

Table 2.3. Major Economic Policy Measures, Initial Policy Responses, and Continued Turmoil

Date/Background	Policy Objectives	Specific Measures
March 1998: Adoption of macrostabilization and financial sector package	Fiscal and monetary: To rebalance macroeconomic policy	• Revised fiscal plan implemented for 1998 aimed at a smaller surplus of ½ percent of GDP, allowing the reinstatement of previously cut social expenditures (of ½–1 percent of GDP) to protect most vulnerable groups • Credit growth of 12–15 percent for 1998 reiterated
	Financial: To safeguard banking system soundness	• Strategy adopted for strengthening regulatory and prudential framework, disclosure standards, and monetary management • Announcement of mergers of finance companies • Announcement of planned improvement of monetary management, with timetable
May 1998: Political and economic turmoil in Indonesia	Monetary: To provide banks with flexibility in liquidity management	• Bank Negara Malaysia began to provide daily reports on its money market operations, including its forecasts of financial system cash flows, its liquidity operations, and money market tender results
June 1998: Increasing signs of policy divergence between prime minister and deputy prime minister	Financial: To lessen the burden in dealing with nonperforming loans	• Danaharta established to purchase the nonperforming loans of financial institutions
July 1998: Evidence of output collapse; equity markets in advanced countries began to decline	Fiscal and monetary: To provide strong stimulus	• National Economic Recovery Plan issued • Additional budgetary and off-budgetary expenditures introduced, aimed at achieving federal government deficit of 2½ percent of GDP • Statutory reserve requirement reduced to 8 percent from 10 percent
	Financial and corporate: To strengthen capital base of financial institutions and resolve bad debt problems	• Danamodal established as a vehicle to recapitalize banks • Corporate Debt Restructuring Committee established to encourage informal arrangement for debt restructuring
August 1998: Russia unilaterally announced debt-service moratorium followed by emergency measures; yen vs. dollar rate plunged; long-term capital management trouble publicized	Monetary: To stimulate economy further and to move gradually to prudential-based system	• Bank Negara Malaysia intervention rate reduced in three steps to 9½ percent from 11 percent • Prudential-based liquidity framework introduced, intended to replace liquid asset requirements by January 2000

financing purchases of real estate and securities. To forestall bank runs and "flight to quality," the government announced a full deposit guarantee in January 1998.

Additional policy measures were put into place between March and August 1998 (Table 2.3). In response to signs of output slowdown, macroeconomic policy was rebalanced in March when fiscal policy was relaxed, whereas the credit policy remained tight relative to the previous trend. Also in March, the authorities adopted a strategy to safeguard the soundness of the financial system. Key measures included the upgrading of capital adequacy, prudential guidelines, and disclosure standards for banking institutions, as well as a merger program for finance companies. These were followed by a comprehensive approach to financial and corporate restructuring through the establishment of the asset management company, Danaharta, in June, and of the recapitalization agency, Danamodal, and the Corporate Debt Restructuring Committee in July. A new liquidity framework for banking institutions was also introduced in July, requiring banks to manage assets and liabilities prudently and efficiently.

Economic Performance Following Initial Policies

Although the financial reform measures would become important to the subsequent improvement of market sentiment, the overall policy package failed to restore confidence right away. Capital outflows continued from early 1997 to mid-1998, estimated at over $10 billion and representing over one-third of end-1996 reserves. The spread between onshore and offshore interest rates widened, suggesting heavy speculation in the currency market. By mid-1998, the ringgit had depreciated by 40 percent, and the stock market had declined by 75 percent from pre-crisis levels. In addition, output contraction was more severe than earlier anticipated, weakening further the financial and corporate sectors. Plagued by increasing nonperforming loans and liquidity constraints, bank lending was reduced beyond the credit plan, which aggravated financial problems in the corporate sector and further brought down investor confidence.

The crisis intensified, in part because of market qualms about the region, but Malaysia's own political uncertainty and insufficient or unclear policies also contributed to the malaise. Investor confidence—already fragile—was shaken by the announcement in late 1997 of a United Engineers Malaysia-Renong deal, which lacked transparency and may have bent stock exchange rules.

From early 1998, the political conflict between the prime minister and the deputy prime minister became more visible and intense, creating doubts about Malaysia's resolve to maintain its policy commitment. In February 1998, it was announced that five financial institutions were in need of recapitalization, but no specific plans for their restructuring was given, sparking renewed concern about financial system vulnerability. The exchange rate and stock markets stabilized briefly around the time that the macroeconomic stabilization and financial sector package was put in place, but instability returned during April–August 1998 following the political turmoil in Indonesia, the fall of the Japanese yen, fears of a devaluation of the Chinese renminbi, and the financial trouble in Russia. Moreover, given the difficulty in recognizing the sharp output slowdown, implementation of countercyclical macroeconomic policies came with considerable delay.[12] Fiscal policy remained relatively tight even after its relaxation in March, and reliance on quantitative monetary targets created problems, as credit was cut from firms that were potentially viable.

As output collapse became evident, macroeconomic policy became more supportive of economic revival. A fiscal stimulus package was launched in August 1998, entailing a significant increase in capital spending and tax reduction, and monetary policy became successively more accommodating.

Exchange and Capital Controls

In September 1998, Malaysia adopted an unorthodox approach that involved exchange and capital controls (Table 2.4) The ringgit was pegged at RM 3.8 per U.S. dollar, restrictions were imposed on the repatriation of portfolio capital, and offshore ringgit activities were prohibited. The strategy was designed to insulate monetary policy from external volatility and facilitate a low interest rate policy, to contain speculative capital movements, to provide certainty to market participants, and to give Malaysia some breathing space needed to carry out structural adjustment.

The market welcomed the financial reform measures and expansionary macroeconomic policies, but the capital controls had an immediate negative impact. Rating agencies downgraded Malaysia, sovereign bond spreads increased relative to those of Korea and Thailand, and Malaysia was removed from major investment indices. This was in part due to investors' uncertainty about the coverage of the controls and the potential impact on foreign direct investment, even though the latter was not to be affected by the controls. Controls on portfolio capital outflows were replaced by a price-based exit levy in February 1999, which was eased and simplified in September 1999 and February 2001 and finally eliminated in May 2001.

Recovery Stage and Recent Performance

The negative impact of capital control measures was nevertheless contained. Regional prospects, which had strengthened just prior to the introduction of capital controls, helped bolster confidence and aided in the recovery process of the crisis countries, including Malaysia. The ringgit turned out, ex post, to have been undervalued, providing a boost to exports and an incentive for retaining funds in the country. Malaysian equities once again became fully liquid following the replacement of quantitative restrictions on their outflows by price-based controls. These equities were reincluded in major investment indices, and portfolio capital returned.

Thus, along with the rest of Asia, Malaysia staged a recovery beginning in 1999: financial sector performance strengthened, investor confidence improved, real output rebounded rapidly, and the inflation rate

---

[12]Macroeconomic restraint at this stage of the crisis was consistent with the policy recommendations of the IMF.

Table 2.4. Major Economic Policy Measures, Exchange and Capital Controls, and Aftermath

Date/Background	Policy Objectives	Specific Measures
September 1998: Deputy prime minister Anwar removed and arrested; Bank Negara Malaysia governor and deputy governor resigned; Malaysia removed from major investment indices causing its sovereign bond spreads to rise as those for other crisis countries fell	Exchange and capital controls: To deter speculation on the ringgit and gain monetary independence	• Ringgit pegged at RM 3.8 per U.S. dollar • Controls on transfers of funds from ringgit-denominated accounts for nonresidents not physically present in Malaysia, in effect imposing a one-year holding period for repatriation of portfolio capital, with retroactive effect • Prohibition of offshore ringgit transactions
	Monetary: To further ease and encourage credit growth	• Reduction of Bank Negara Malaysia intervention rate to 8 percent from 9½ percent; modification of formula to link base lending rate to policy rate; reduction in statutory reserve requirement in two steps to 4 percent from 8 percent; reduction in liquid asset ratio requirement to 15 percent from 17 percent • Individual banks' minimum loan growth target set at 8 percent; relaxation of restrictions introduced in early 1997 on bank lending to purchase property and shares • Prudential regulations regarding nonperforming loans and disclosure requirements relaxed
October 1998–August 1999	Fiscal and monetary: To stimulate economic activity	• Announcement of 1999 federal government budget aimed at achieving deficit of 5½ percent of GDP • Successive reductions of Bank Negara Malaysia intervention rate to 7½ percent (10/98), to 7 percent (11/98), to 6½ percent (4/99), to 6 percent (5/99), and to 5.5 percent (8/99)
January 1999	Monetary: To contain investment in selected activities	• New lending for residential development above a certain threshold was restricted by Bank Negara Malaysia
January–March 1999	Corporate: To adopt best practices	• Various measures to enhance disclosure for listed companies and to restrict the number of directorships held by an individual • Report of High Level Finance Committee on Corporate Governance released to the public
February 1999: After the easing of capital controls, spreads narrowed and plans to include Malaysia once again in investment indices announced	Capital controls: To preempt exodus of capital and reengage foreign investors	• Easing of some controls, including replacement of 12-month holding period for repatriation of portfolio capital by system of a graduated exit levy
April 1999	Financial: To strengthen supervision and regulation	• Measures included intensified supervision, performance reviews for bank CEOs, elimination of two-tier bank classification, and disallowing of bank lending to controlling shareholders
September 1999	Capital controls: To provide further relaxation	• Graduated exit levy on portfolio investment simplified and replaced by a flat 10 percent levy on repatriation of profits • Some relaxation in swap and forward transactions for the purpose of share purchases
November 1999: Malaysia reincluded in Dow Jones/IFC investment indices	Financial: To strengthen management and supervision	• Risk-based supervision initiated, with consultation between Bank Negara Malaysia and banks regarding minimum guidelines on credit risk-management practices

Table 2.4 *(concluded)*

Date/Background	Policy Objectives	Specific Measures
February 2000	Capital controls: To resolve pending issue	• Resolution on Central Limit Order Book that froze investors' Kuala Lumpur Stock Exchange shares traded in Singapore as from 9/98
April 2000: Malaysia reincluded in Morgan Stanley Capital International investment index (May)	Capital markets: To develop	• Announcement of consolidation of stockbroking companies, to 15 by end-2000 from 63 (deadline later extended) • National Bond Market Committee established to provide policy direction and rationalize regulatory framework for bond market development
October 2000	Fiscal: To put in place another stimulus budget Capital controls: To provide further easing	• Announcement of 2001 budget aimed at achieving federal government deficit of 4½ percent • Proposal to remove 10 percent exit levy on portfolio capital profits repatriated after one year (effective 2/01)

fell. A large external current account surplus and reduced capital outflows allowed a buildup of international reserves that continued until mid-2000. Although the real effective rate of the ringgit has appreciated in recent months, it remained broadly stable throughout 1999–2000, as exchange rates of trading partners that had also been affected by the crisis began to stabilize at about the same time as the pegging of the ringgit. Indications are that the ringgit has moved close to its fair value by March–April 2001.

Reflecting better market sentiment, the Kuala Lumpur stock exchange price index surged, after having bottomed out, also around September 1998. As in the other crisis countries, the index has continued to fluctuate along with stock prices in major markets, especially in the United States, which have softened significantly since early 2000. Spreads for Malaysian sovereign bonds declined from their peak in September 1998, even if they have edged up in recent months.

Bank balance sheets have improved, reflecting both the economic turnaround and the achievements of Danaharta, Danamodal, and the Corporate Debt Restructuring Committee, which have allowed banks to be rid of nonperforming loans and to strengthen their capital base, and have allowed corporate debt to be removed. There are indications that Malaysia has moved ahead of other crisis countries in respect to formulation of prudential regulation, resolution of nonperforming loans, restoration of capital adequacy, and implementation of a bank consolidation program, all of which have helped reinforce investor confidence that the economy was undergoing fundamental adjustment.

There are indications, however, that the performance of Malaysian corporations, which had been more profitable and under less financial stress prior to the crisis than that of their counterparts in Korea and Thailand, deteriorated to a greater extent during the crisis and has recently fared no better than the others. Similar to the other countries, operational restructuring of the corporate sector has been slow and, reportedly, has not adhered fully to best corporate governance practices.

Appendix. Graphical Overview of Indicators During Precrisis, Crisis, and Recovery

Figure A.2.1. Selected Asian Countries: Precrisis Macroeconomic Indicators

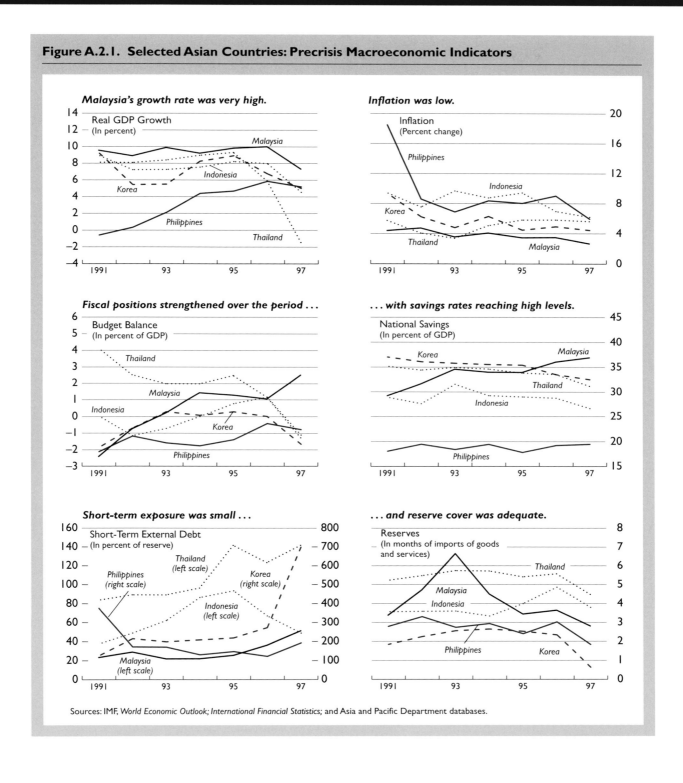

Sources: IMF, *World Economic Outlook; International Financial Statistics;* and Asia and Pacific Department databases.

Figure A.2.2. Selected Asian Countries: Precrisis Financial Indicators

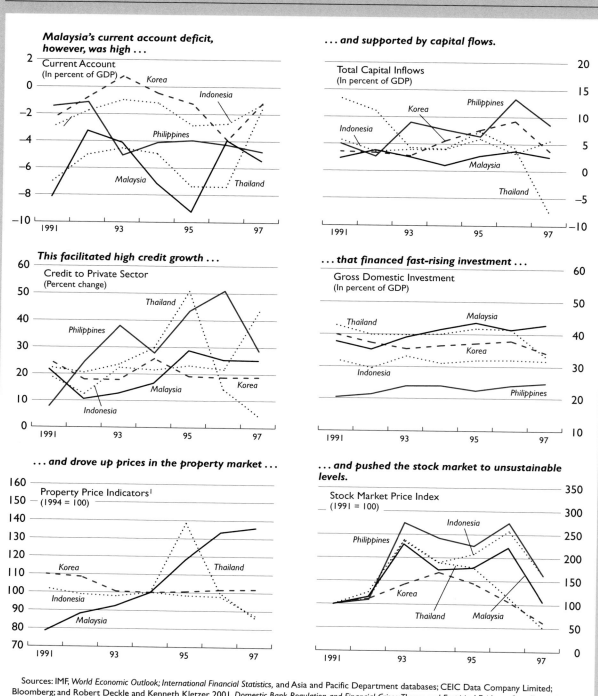

Sources: IMF, *World Economic Outlook; International Financial Statistics,* and Asia and Pacific Department databases; CEIC Data Company Limited; Bloomberg; and Robert Deckle and Kenneth Kletzer 2001, *Domestic Bank Regulation and Financial Crises: Theory and Empirical Evidence from East Asia, IMF Working Paper 01/63* (Washington: International Monetary Fund).

[1]House price index for Malaysia, real estate price for Thailand, and construction value index for Indonesia. Data are not available for Philippines.

Figure A.2.3. Selected Asian Countries: Economic Indicators During the Crisis Period

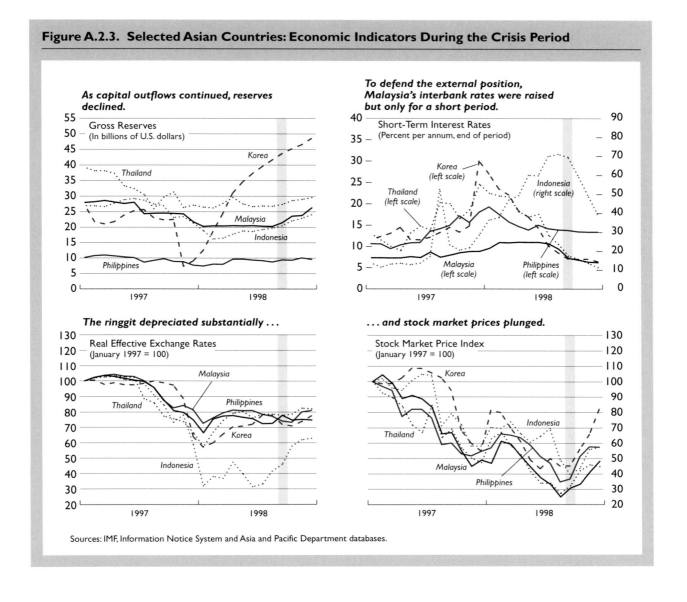

As capital outflows continued, reserves declined.

Gross Reserves
(In billions of U.S. dollars)

Korea

Thailand

Malaysia

Indonesia

Philippines

1997   1998

To defend the external position, Malaysia's interbank rates were raised but only for a short period.

Short-Term Interest Rates
(Percent per annum, end of period)

Korea
(left scale)

Indonesia
(right scale)

Thailand
(left scale)

Malaysia
(left scale)

Philippines
(left scale)

1997   1998

The ringgit depreciated substantially . . .

Real Effective Exchange Rates
(January 1997 = 100)

Malaysia

Thailand

Philippines

Korea

Indonesia

1997   1998

. . . and stock market prices plunged.

Stock Market Price Index
(January 1997 = 100)

Korea

Indonesia

Thailand

Malaysia

Philippines

1997   1998

Sources: IMF, Information Notice System and Asia and Pacific Department databases.

Figure A.2.4. Selected Asian Countries: Economic Developments

Domestic demand in Malaysia began to weaken in the second half of 1997, and remained subdued until late 1999.

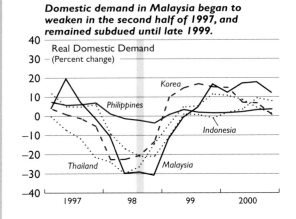

Real Domestic Demand
(Percent change)

Output collapsed in the first quarter of 1998 and continued down through that year.

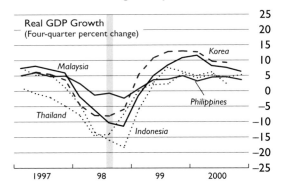

Real GDP Growth
(Four-quarter percent change)

The weak domestic demand was consistent with tight fiscal policy in effect until late 1998.

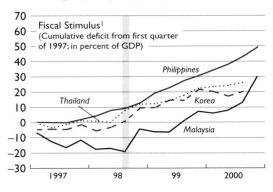

Fiscal Stimulus[1]
(Cumulative deficit from first quarter of 1997; in percent of GDP)

Credit growth also declined sharply, beyond credit plans, in response to the weakening corporate sector and rising nonperforming loans.

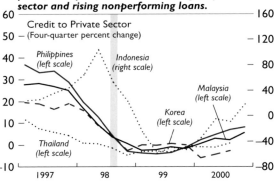

Credit to Private Sector
(Four-quarter percent change)

Sources: IMF, Asia and Pacific Department databases; and CEIC Data Company Limited.
[1]Data are not available for Indonesia.

Figure A.2.5. Selected Asian Countries: Financial Market Indicators During the Crisis Period

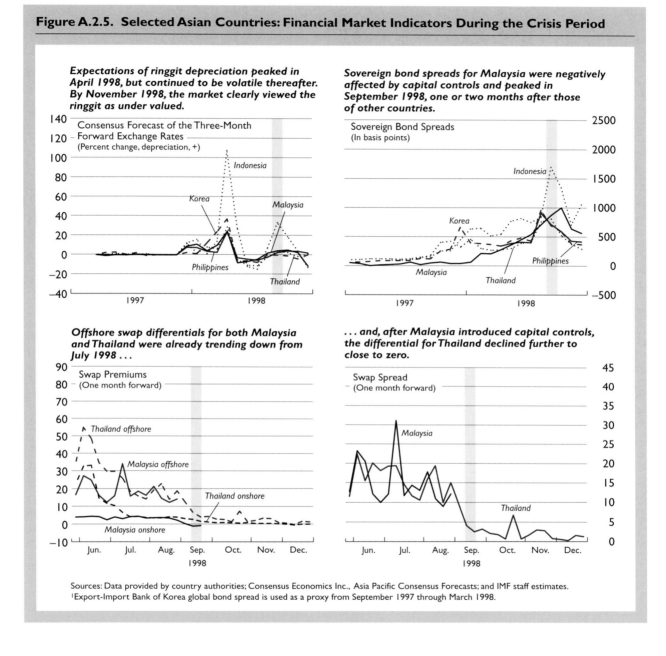

Expectations of ringgit depreciation peaked in April 1998, but continued to be volatile thereafter. By November 1998, the market clearly viewed the ringgit as under valued.

Consensus Forecast of the Three-Month Forward Exchange Rates
(Percent change, depreciation, +)

Indonesia
Korea
Malaysia
Philippines
Thailand

1997   1998

Sovereign bond spreads for Malaysia were negatively affected by capital controls and peaked in September 1998, one or two months after those of other countries.

Sovereign Bond Spreads
(In basis points)

Indonesia
Korea
Malaysia
Thailand
Philippines

1997   1998

Offshore swap differentials for both Malaysia and Thailand were already trending down from July 1998 . . .

Swap Premiums
(One month forward)

Thailand offshore
Malaysia offshore
Thailand onshore
Malaysia onshore

Jun.   Jul.   Aug.   Sep.   Oct.   Nov.   Dec.
1998

. . . and, after Malaysia introduced capital controls, the differential for Thailand declined further to close to zero.

Swap Spread
(One month forward)

Malaysia
Thailand

Jun.   Jul.   Aug.   Sep.   Oct.   Nov.   Dec.
1998

Sources: Data provided by country authorities; Consensus Economics Inc., Asia Pacific Consensus Forecasts; and IMF staff estimates.
[1]Export-Import Bank of Korea global bond spread is used as a proxy from September 1997 through March 1998.

Figure A.2.6. Selected Asian Countries: Economic Performance During the Recovery Stage

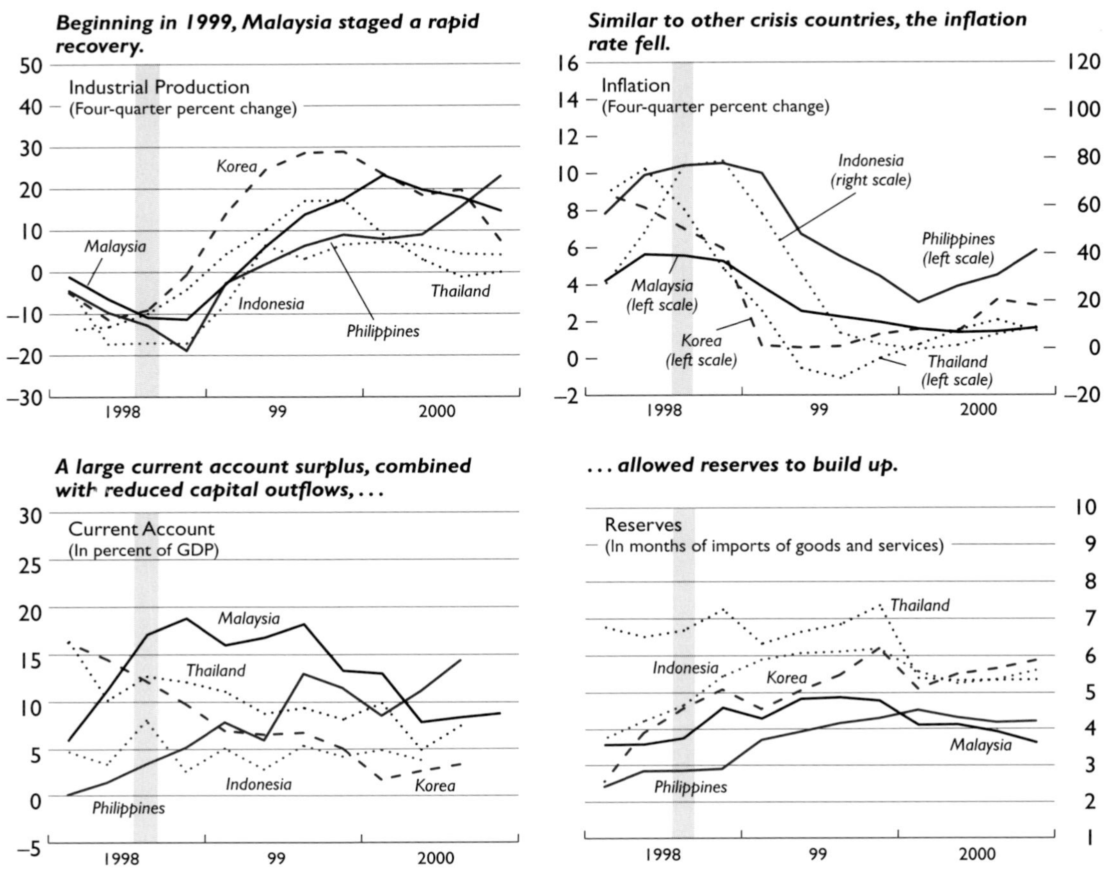
Beginning in 1999, Malaysia staged a rapid recovery.
Industrial Production
(Four-quarter percent change)
50
40
30
20
10
0
–10
–20
–30
Korea
Malaysia
Indonesia
Thailand
Philippines
1998
99
2000
Similar to other crisis countries, the inflation rate fell.
Inflation
(Four-quarter percent change)
16
14
12
10
8
6
4
2
0
–2
120
100
80
60
40
20
0
–20
Indonesia
(right scale)
Philippines
(left scale)
Malaysia
(left scale)
Korea
(left scale)
Thailand
(left scale)
1998
99
2000
A large current account surplus, combined with reduced capital outflows, . . .
Current Account
(In percent of GDP)
30
25
20
15
10
5
0
–5
Malaysia
Thailand
Indonesia
Korea
Philippines
1998
99
2000
. . . allowed reserves to build up.
Reserves
(In months of imports of goods and services)
10
9
8
7
6
5
4
3
2
1
Thailand
Indonesia
Korea
Malaysia
Philippines
1998
99
2000

Sources: IMF, *International Financial Statistics*; and Asia and Pacific Department databases.

Figure A.2.7. Selected Asian Countries: Financial Indicators During the Recovery Stage

Real effective exchange rate for Malaysia remained broadly stable throughout 1999–2000.

The stock market performance in all crisis countries improved, peaked in early 2000, then softened in line with the U.S. equity market.

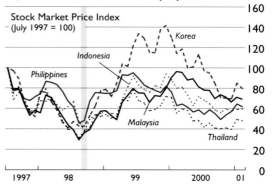

Spreads for Malaysia declined and stayed low, close to those for Korea and Thailand.

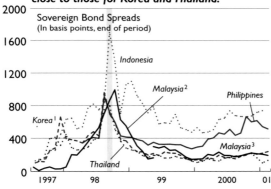

Sources: IMF, Information Notice System; Bloomberg; and Asia and Pacific Department databases.
[1]Export-Import Bank of Korea global bond spread is used as a proxy from September 1997 through March 1998.
[2]Sovereign bond issued September 19, 1990 that matured on September 27, 2000.
[3]Sovereign bond issued May 26, 1999 and maturing on June 1, 2009.

Figure A.2.8. Selected Asian Countries: Fiscal Indicators

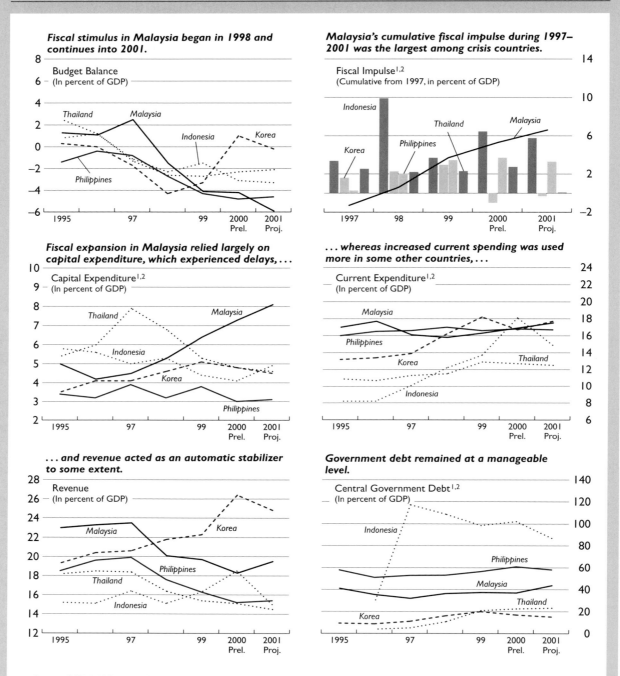

Sources: IMF, *World Economic Outlook*; *International Financial Statistics*; and Asia and Pacific Department databases.
[1]For Indonesia, 1995 through 1999 are on a fiscal year basis (fiscal year ending March). Year 2000 contains data for three quarters. Figure for 2001 is on a calendar year basis.
[2]Thailand is on a fiscal year basis (fiscal year ending September).

Figure A.2.9. Selected Asian Countries: Monetary Indicators

Interest rates in Malaysia were kept lower than in other countries for the greater part of the crisis, . . .

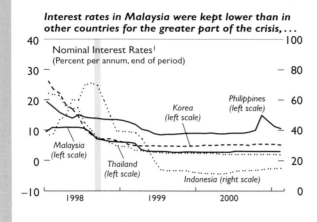

Nominal Interest Rates[1]
(Percent per annum, end of period)

Philippines (left scale)

Korea (left scale)

Malaysia (left scale)

Thailand (left scale)

Indonesia (right scale)

. . . both in nominal and real terms, mitigating corporate financial distress.

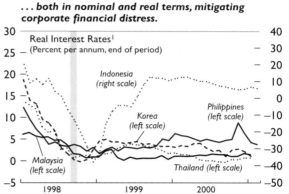

Real Interest Rates[1]
(Percent per annum, end of period)

Indonesia (right scale)

Korea (left scale)

Philippines (left scale)

Malaysia (left scale)

Thailand (left scale)

But, similar to other countries, private credit growth in Malaysia remained subdued and did not meet the authorities' target for 1999 or 2000.

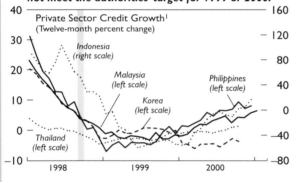

Private Sector Credit Growth[1]
(Twelve-month percent change)

Indonesia (right scale)

Malaysia (left scale)

Korea (left scale)

Philippines (left scale)

Thailand (left scale)

Sources: *International Financial Statistics*; and Asia and Pacific Department databases.
[1]Temporary capital controls introduced in September 1998.

III   Potential Output and Inflation

Il Houng Lee and Yougesh Khatri

Two groups of methods may be used to estimate potential output. One group is based on statistical techniques that attempt to decompose a time series into the permanent and cyclical components; the other group is based on estimating structural relationships, which in turn are usually obtained from economic theory. Potential output is estimated for Malaysia using the cubic spline-smoothing method where the result indicates that the output gap would close toward end-2000 or early 2001. Thereafter, inflation is forecasted using the estimated output gap as one of its determinants.

Introduction

Potential output is an important input to macroeconomic policy design. For practical purposes, potential output can be defined as the maximum output an economy can sustain without generating an increase in inflation. The output gap is simply the difference between actual and potential output. In the short run, estimates of the output gap provide a key indicator of inflationary pressures. This section estimates potential output for Malaysia using various approaches applied to data through end-1999; then inflation is forecast using the estimated output gap as one of its determinants. The different approaches used are briefly outlined,[1] an estimate of potential output in Malaysia and the implied output gap are provided, followed by an inflation equation estimated using the output gap.

To summarize, of the several approaches available, the potential output estimated using the cubic spline-smoothing method appears to provide the most plausible result, ex post, in terms of the implied output gap. Estimates suggest the gap is expected to close in late 2000 or early 2001, implying that inflationary pressures could start building up in the near future. The estimated inflation equation confirms that inflation would rise above 3 percent (year-on-year) during 2000 if the gap were to close.[2]

Measuring Potential Output

The concept of potential output is not well defined and is difficult to measure. The literature broadly suggests two definitions (see Scacciavillani and Swagel, 1999). The first arises from the assumption that the business cycle results mainly from movements in aggregate demand in relation to a slowly moving level of aggregate supply. This occasions (potentially substantial) swings during which there are overutilized/underutilized resources.

The second definition follows the neoclassical tradition, where potential output is assumed to be driven by exogenous productivity shocks to aggregate supply that determine long-run growth and, to a large extent, short-term fluctuation in output over the business cycle.[3] According to the latter approach, output fluctuates around its potential level but generally without wide or prolonged divergence.

Potential output is an unobservable variable, making it difficult to measure. In practice, there are a plethora of techniques, each with advantages and drawbacks, and no single methodology dominates. These techniques could be classified broadly into two groups.

The first group of methods is purely statistical and attempts to decompose a time series into permanent and cyclical components. This category would include filtering methods (moving averages, the Hodrick-Prescott (HP) filter, the Beveridge-Nelson method, Kernel estimators, and spline-smoothing

---

[1]A more technical exposition is contained in the Appendix.

[2]Discussions below on the problems of the structural break in 1998 and the use of end-period data in 1999 (which is still a point in the recovery path) highlight the tentative nature of this estimation, carried out in April 2000. The results should thus be viewed as indicative. The latest data together with the expected slowdown in 2001 suggest that the gap may now persist into 2002.

[3]In such a case, business cycles are not necessarily driven by shortfalls or excesses of aggregate demand, but rather by rational agents reacting to productivity shocks by writing off old investments and reinvesting in new opportunities.

techniques) and unobservable component methods (both univariate and multivariate approaches). Most of these approaches derive the permanent component as a trend by minimizing the distance between the points on the trend and the actual value at prespecified intervals, while penalizing frequent changes of the second moments of the estimated trend in order to ensure some degree of smoothness of the estimated trend. Although these approaches are attractive, in that they require considerably less data than other methods, they become ill-defined at the beginning and end of samples, or if there is a structural break in the data.

The second group of methods is based on estimating structural relationships, including production functions, multivariate systems of equations, structural vector autoregressions (VARs), and "demand-side" models. The production function methodology represents the middle ground between a full-scale structural model and the various univariate approaches (such as filters and unobservable components). Even then, this approach is considerably more demanding in terms of data requirements than filtering approaches, and the nature of inputs data—particularly the capital stock calculations—implies significant potential measurement errors in inputs.[4] The demand-side approach relates output directly to measures of spare capacity in the economy or supply-side measures. The structural VAR approach combines aggregate supply (and supply shocks) and cyclical fluctuations with changes in aggregate demand using a structural VAR with restrictions imposed on the long-run effects of impacts on output and unemployment. These long-run restrictions are used to identify structural supply and demand shocks by allowing supply shocks to have a permanent effect on output, while demand shocks are assumed to have only a temporary effect on output.[5]

Estimating the Output Gap

Of the approaches outlined above (and described more fully in the Appendix), a univariate filtering

technique, namely the cubic spline-smoothing method (CSSM), was chosen to estimate the potential output for Malaysia. The main reason for selecting this approach was its simplicity, especially relating to data requirements. A production function approach was also tried, but it did not indicate an improvement over results obtained from filtering techniques. The CSSM was preferred over other filtering techniques as it rendered the most plausible potential output path in terms of the implied output gap, especially in relation to actual inflation.[6]

There are two weaknesses that need to be addressed using any of the smoothing methods: the structural break in the GDP series, due to the sharp decline in output in 1998; and the end-period problems. Given the structural break in 1998, smoothing methods tend to underweight the GDP growth in 1997, implying a positive output gap, even though there was no evidence of overheating (e.g., no inflationary pressures were noted in 1997). Furthermore, the end-point of actual data, i.e., end-1999, which is still a point in the recovery path, tends to bring down the estimated potential output such that the estimated output gaps in 1998–99 are small. In view of the magnitude of output decline in 1998 with no apparent physical damage or dramatic shift in the structure of demand that would make existing capital redundant on a permanent basis, the low output gap during the postcrisis period does not appear to be consistent with the actual unutilized productive capacity of the economy.

To address these issues, an interpolated point was used for 1998 (instead of actual), and the sample period was extended to 2002 using the 1998 IMF *World Economic Outlook* (WEO) forecast.[7] Annual data were used for the period covering 1970–2002. The estimated output gap, adjusted for these two weaknesses (Adj. SP), is compared with the gap estimated without the interpolated point (Figure 3.1) in 1998 using the CSSM (SP), the HP filter (with values of $\lambda=7$ (HP7) and $\lambda=100$ (HP100)), the Kernel smoothing method (KN), and the production function (PF). As is shown in Table 3.1, except for the adjusted CSSM, other smoothing methods tend to overstate the degree of overheating during the precrisis period while understating the output gap during the postcrisis period. The degree of over- and underestimation is made worse by the extension of the end-period through 2003.

---

[4]At the IMF, the production function approach has been applied mainly to industrial countries (see De Masi, 1997). Relatively few empirical studies attempt to estimate potential output for developing countries, mainly due to a lack of reliable data. Also, the concept of potential output may be less relevant when a large fraction of output relates to primary commodities, whose production is supply-determined, or where there are large migration-related flows of labor and ongoing structural change (associated with the "catch-up" phase of development).

[5]In multivariate unobserved component models or structural VARs, the relationship between inflation and output implicit in the definition of potential output can be imposed during the estimation of potential output (Dupasquier, Guay, and St. Amant, 1999; Apel and Jansson, 1999; Scacciavillani and Swagel, 1999; and Cerra and Saxena, 2000).

[6]The λ was determined according to the generalized cross-validation criteria.

[7]The CSSM was first used to estimate the 1998 value, which was omitted from the series as missing and interpolated, then the CSSM was used on the new series with the interpolated 1998 value to obtain potential output.

Figure 3.1. Comparing Estimates of Output Gap With (Adj. SP) and Without (SP) the Interpolated Point in 1998
(Changes in Log (Index))

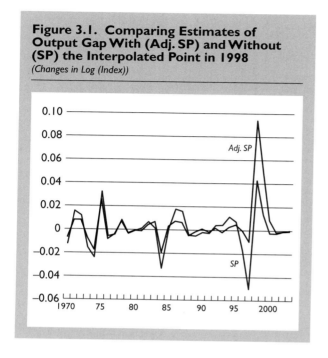

The output gap, estimated using the production function, does not indicate an improvement over results obtained from filtering techniques. This reflects in part the fact that smoothing techniques were used to derive the potential labor force (i.e., at a nonaccelerating inflation rate of unemployment (NAIRU) consistent level) and the trend total factor productivity (TFP) growth. This implies shifting the problems associated with estimation of trend GDP one layer down to estimation of trend labor force and total factor productivity growth.[8]

Determinants of Inflation

Studies have used various approaches to modeling inflation, depending on the structure of the country and objectives of the analysis. Approaches from the supply side include markup models, where the general domestic price level is estimated as a markup over total unit costs, including labor costs, import prices, and energy prices (see de Brouwer and Ericsson, 1998). Another approach centers around a money market equation, sometimes to-

gether with an explicit equation for purchasing power parity (PPP) (e.g., Jonsson, 1999). In other studies, the external sector disequilibrium pressure is measured using the difference between actual and estimated equilibrium exchange rates (Lim and Papi, 1997). Single-equation models include some form of expectation-augmented Phillips curve (Razzak, 1995; and Stock and Watson, 1999). A more formal structural approach involves various combinations of the above, where, for example, Chhibber and others (1989) introduce PPP (for traded goods), markup (for nontraded goods), and allowances made for controlled prices.

The approach adopted in this section is eclectic and tries to capture the key sources of inflationary pressures in Malaysia. The pressure exerted on prices by excess domestic demand or supply shocks (through the output gap) is dampened to the extent that some of the pressure is released through adjustments in imports. Changes in imports as a percent of GDP, therefore, would play a role in determining inflation. Furthermore, the PPP condition is introduced to accommodate the impact of foreign prices and the exchange rate on domestic inflation. Specifically:

$$p = f(gap, img, ex, wp), \qquad (1)$$

where p = domestic price; gap = output gap; img = imports as a share of GDP; ex = nominal effective exchange rate; and wp = foreign price.

The estimation methodology is the familiar maximum likelihood cointegration procedure by Johansen. The long-run relationship is estimated using the VAR on p, img, ex, and wp. The short-run dynamics are estimated using an error-correction mechanism (ECM), in which we introduce the output gap, and inflation is forecast 12 months ahead (through 2001Q1). Inflation is projected to reach 3½ percent to 4 percent (year-on-year) by the first quarter of 2001, although, given the short observation period, the result obtained needs to be interpreted with caution.

Data

Data are quarterly, covering 1991 (Q1) through 2000 (Q1), although the ECM is estimated for 1991–99.

- p: domestic price is defined as the logarithm of the consumer price index. As there are no detailed breakdowns of the consumer price index for the specified period, no adjustments are made for transitory fluctuations or rigidities that are controlled or influenced by the government.

- img: the ratio is defined as merchandise imports to GDP.

---

[8]Bank Negara Malaysia's estimate of potential output in early 2000, based on a production function, found that the output gap was narrowing and potential output was back on its growth path (Bank Negara Malaysia, 1999).

Table 3.1. Estimates of Output Gap, 1996–2001

	Adj. SP	SP	HP7	HP100	KN	PF
1996	0.04	1.62	4.17	7.45	0.47	5.47
1997	0.97	4.93	6.69	9.10	4.45	5.49
1998	−9.39	−4.25	−4.70	−3.87	−3.98	−6.21
1999	−4.94	−1.32	−3.06	−3.47	−0.26	−4.31
2000	−0.86	0.23	−1.36	−2.31	0.05	…
2001	0.15	0.20	−0.59	−1.45	−0.18	…

- *ex*: the nominal effective exchange rate index is defined as the log of the nominal effective exchange rate and is derived from trading partners weighted by their relative trade share (IMF, IFS).

- *wp*: foreign price is defined as the log of an index derived as a composite of price indices of the United States (30 percent), Japan (20 percent), Singapore (20 percent), Germany (15 percent), and the United Kingdom (15 percent) (IMF, IFS).

- *gap*: output gap is defined as actual output divided by potential output. The potential output is obtained using spline-smoothing allowing for the structural break during parts of 1998 and 1999 and using the same approach as elaborated above, but using quarterly data. Hence, *gap* < 1 implies excess capacity.

Integration and Cointegration

Statistical tests indicate that all variables are integrated of order two or lower. In particular, according to the Augmented Dickey-Fuller (ADF) statistic, *p* appears to be I(1), and the other three variables appear to be I(2). However, their estimated coefficients are numerically much less than unity, i.e., the coefficients of Δimg, Δex, and Δwp are $(-0.14 = 1 - 1.14)$, $(-0.04 = 1 - 0.96)$, and $(0.33 = 1 - 0.67)$, respectively. Thus, all four variables are treated below as if they are I(1).[9]

The Johansen maximum likelihood estimation procedure for finite-order VARs is used to obtain the long-run relationship between integrated variables. As there was no a priori information on the lag order of the VAR, a fourth-order VAR was used and simplified to a first-order VAR on the basis of the results presented in Table 3.2, below.

---

[9]See de Brouwer and Ericsson (1998) for a similar approach.

Table 3.3 reports the result of VAR(1) on *g*, *m*, *img*, *ex*, and *wp*. As indicated by the Johansen maximal eigenvalue (λmax) and trace eigenvalue (λtrace) statistics, the result rejects the null hypothesis of no cointegration in favor of at least one cointegrating relationship. The rows of the β matrix in Table 3.3 can be interpreted as long-run parameters and the elements in the matrix α as adjustment coefficients (see Charemza and Deadman, 1992).

The first row of β, which is the estimated cointegrating vector, represents a long-run relationship between the variables estimated and can be expressed as:

$$p = \text{constant} - 0.0214 \, img - 0.1029 \, ex$$
$$+ 1.8302 \, wp \qquad (2)$$

All of the estimated coefficients have the right signs and explain that Malaysia's price index declines with larger imports as a percent of GDP and with an appreciation of the nominal effective exchange rate, but increases with higher world prices. Having established a long-run relationship, a single equation model is used to assess the short-term behavior of the price level.

The Short-Run Dynamics of Inflation

An unrestricted error-correction model is used to examine the dynamics of inflation in the short run. It incorporates the long-run relationship obtained above as follows:

$$\Delta p_t = a_0 + \Sigma b_{1j}\Delta p_{t-j} + \Sigma b_{2i}\Delta img_{t-i}$$
$$+ \Sigma b_{3i}\Delta ex_{t-i} + \Sigma b_{4i}\Delta wp_{t-i}$$
$$+ a_1 res_{t-1} + a_2 S_t + a_2 D_t + v_t, \qquad (3)$$

where $i = (0, 1, 2, 3, 4)$ and $j = (1, 2, 3)$; "*res*" is obtained from $p - p(\text{est})$, where $p(\text{est})$ is obtained from (2) above; *S* denotes the seasonal dummies; and *D* is a dummy variable to capture the structural break

Table 3.2. F and SC Statistics for Sequential Reduction from VAR(4) to VAR(1)

System	k[2]	Null Hypothesis Log Likelihood	SC[3]	Maintained Hypothesis[1] VAR(4)	VAR(3)	VAR(2)
VAR(4)	68	639.5	−32.60			
VAR(3)	52	622.2	−33.26	0.988 (0.489)		
VAR(2)	36	599.1	−33.54	1.409 (0.143)	1.873 (0.047)	
VAR(1)	20	583.5	−34.30	1.488 (0.086)	1.755 (0.030)	1.445 (0.151)

[1]The numbers represent F-statistics for testing the null hypothesis against the maintained hypothesis, and the tail probability associated with that value of the F-statistics (in parentheses).
[2]Number of unrestricted parameters.
[3]Schwartz criterion.

Table 3.3. Cointegration Analysis of Price Data, 1991Q2 to 2000Q1[1]

Ho:rank=p	λmax	95%	λtrace	95%
P == 0	30.0[2]	27.1	54.9[3]	47.2
P <= 1	15.8	21.0	24.9	29.7
P <= 2	6.3	14.1	9.1	15.4
P <= 3	2.9	3.8	2.9	3.8

Standardized β eigenvectors

	p	img	ex	wp
	1.000	0.021	0.102	−1.829
	−1.443	1.000	−1.044	−1.713
	−42.747	−10.621	1.000	78.069
	−0.739	0.569	0.217	1.000

Standardized α coefficients

p	−0.236	0.016	0.001	0.009
img	−0.554	−0.051	0.011	−0.186
ex	1.609	0.164	−0.008	−0.108
wp	0.166	0.001	0.001	0.004

[1]PcFiml 9.0 for Windows was used to estimate the VAR.
[2]Significant at the 95 percent level.
[3]Significant at the 99 percent level.

during 1998. Again, using OLS, the order of lags are reduced in sequence, and the following variables were retained:[10]

---

[10]Although not reported here, the F and SC statistics were used to test the null hypothesis during the sequence of eliminating variables. The latter are selected according to the lowest *t*-values at each stage of the OLS estimations.

$\Delta p_{t-2}, \Delta img_{t-3}, \Delta ex_{t-2}, \Delta ex_{t-2}, \Delta wp_{t-3},$
$\Delta gap_t, gap_{t-1}, and res_{t-1}.$

Using the estimated coefficients as reported in Table 3.4, inflation is forecast for the 12 months through 2001Q1. The projection indicates an upward trend in inflation, reaching 3½ percent to 4 percent during 2000Q1. The result is presented in Figures 3.2 and 3.3, below.

Table 3.4. Result of Inflation Estimation by OLS, 1992Q2–1999Q4[1]

The present sample is: 1992 (2) to 1999 (4)

Variable	Coefficient	Std. error	t-value	t-prob	Part R^2
Constant	0.046055	0.027674	1.664	0.1096	0.1075
Dp_{t-2}	−0.26606	0.14359	−1.853	0.0768	0.1299
$Dimg_{t-3}$	0.028043	0.016735	1.676	0.1073	0.1088
Dex_{t-2}	−0.018984	0.015673	−1.211	0.2381	0.0600
Dwp_{t-3}	0.77974	0.24717	3.155	0.0044	0.3020
$Dgap_t$	−0.11003	0.047982	−2.293	0.0313	0.1861
Gap_{t-1}	−0.039224	0.027506	−1.426	0.1673	0.0812
Res_{t-1}	−0.016748	0.083422	−0.201	0.8426	0.0017

R^2 = 0.690712 F(7,23) = 7.3378 [0.0001] \sigma = 0.00348159 DW = 2.53

RSS = 0.0002787939991 for 8 variables and 31 observations

[1]PcGive was used to estimate the equation;"D" represents first difference.

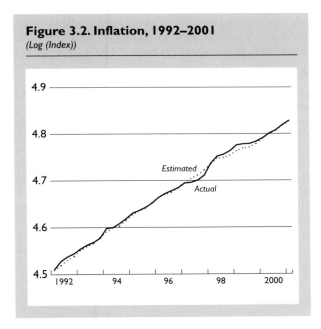

Figure 3.2. Inflation, 1992–2001
(Log (Index))

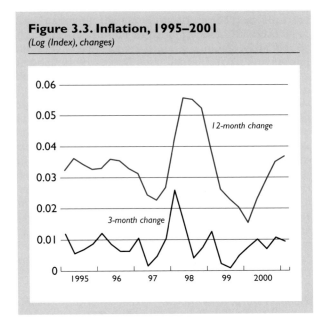

Figure 3.3. Inflation, 1995–2001
(Log (Index), changes)

Appendix. Approaches to Measuring Potential Output

Potential output is defined as the maximum output an economy can sustain without generating an increase in inflation. There are two groups of methods that may be used to estimate the potential output. One group is based on statistical techniques that attempt to decompose a time series into permanent and cyclical components; the other group is based on estimating structural relationships based on economic theory. Below, the various methodologies are outlined and some of their main attributes and drawbacks are highlighted. Detailed descriptions of the methodologies can be found in the studies cited.

Statistical Filters and Smoothing Methods

Simple Trends

The simplest method of estimating potential output is the use of a linear time trend. This can be refined by using spline trends to allow for structural breaks or by including a polynomial in the trend term to allow for nonlinearity (for an example, see Bayoumi and others, 1999).

The main attraction of using a simple time trend or variants thereof is its simplicity. Since the publication of an influential paper by Nelson and Plosser (1982), however, which suggested that output series are best characterized as integrated series, there has been increasing recognition that measuring the permanent component of output, i.e., potential output, with any degree of accuracy is a difficult task. In particular, the existence of a stochastic permanent component implies that potential output cannot be treated as a deterministic trend (Dupasquier, Guay, and St. Amant, 1999).[11]

The Hodrick-Prescott (HP) and Other Filters

Filters and smoothing methodologies can be as simple as a moving average. More complex smoothing techniques include the HP filter, which chooses trend output, y^*, such that, for a given parameter λ (which determines the degree of smoothness), the sum of squared deviations of y from y^* plus λ times the sum of the rate of change of y^* is minimized. Mathematically, trend output, y^*, is derived for a given λ by:

$$Min \left[\sum_{t=0}^{T} (y_t - y_t^*)^2 + \lambda \sum_{t=2}^{T-1} (\Delta^2 y_{t+1}^*)^2 \right], \qquad (4)$$

where Δ^2 indicates twice differencing. The larger the parameter λ, the more weight given to smoothness (determined by the second term) versus fit (determined by the first term). For a discussion of the statistical properties of the HP filter, see Cogley and Nason (1995), Harvey and Jaeger (1993), and Soderlind (1994).

- The HP and other such filters are attractive because considerably less data are required than for other methods such as the production function, unobservable variables, or structural VARs, discussed below. Use of these filters, however, has certain disadvantages.

- The resultant measure of output depends critically on the choice of the smoothing parameter, λ.[12] The smoothing parameter, in effect, determines the "window" of data used to calculate the trend; the larger the smoothing parameter, the broader this window of data used and the smoother the trend.

- The HP filter can induce spurious cyclicality in the smoothed series when the series are integrated or nearly integrated[13] (see Harvey and Jaeger, 1993; and Cogley and Nason, 1995).

- Probably the most serious drawback of filtering methods for policymaking purposes is that they become ill defined at the beginning and end of samples; see, for example, Baxter and King (1995), who recommend discarding three years of quarterly data at both ends of a sample. This is a significant drawback for those policymakers wishing to use the measure of the current output gap and thus focus on the most recent observations.[14]

- The HP and other such filtering methods also tend to neglect structural breaks and regime shifts (Scacciavillani and Swagel, 1999).

The Coe-McDermott Method

Coe and McDermott (1997) use a nonparametric (Kernel) smoothing technique, essentially similar to the HP filter but where the degree of smoothness (in the case of the Kernel estimator, determined by the bandwidth (h), similar to the HP λ in determining the "window" of data used for the smoothing) is determined by the data, hence addressing one of the major problems associated with the HP filter. Details of the methodology can be found in the appendix to Coe and McDermott (1997), and a general discussion of nonparametric techniques is provided by Härdle (1990). The method, however, is still likely to share the other problems of the HP filter.

Running Median Smoothing (RMS)

A simple form of the RMS filter uses a running window on the data, the smoothed value in each period being set equal to the median of the values in the window. The method can be extended to apply multiple passes and to use different sizes of data

---

[11]The time trend was traditionally included in equations explaining output as a measure of exogenous technical change. With growing awareness of the importance of the time series properties of variables being modeled (and particularly of the regression residuals in the case of cointegrating regressions), the use of the time trend has diminished. Some studies use direct measures of factors affecting technical change, such as research and development or human capital proxies, to account for technical change (see, for example, Adams and Coe, 1990).

[12]The choice of λ depends on the frequency of the data. For quarterly data, HP set $\lambda=1600$. Correspondingly, for annual and

monthly data, λ might be set to 7 and 126400, respectively (see Microfit 4 Manual). For annual data, setting $\lambda=100$ has the effect of removing output cycles from the data with frequencies less than eight years (Scacciavillani and Swagel, 1999).

[13]Guay and St. Amant (1996) find that the HP filter performs poorly in identifying cyclical components of time series that have a spectrum or pseudo-spectrum with Granger's typical shape, which is that of most macroeconomic time series.

[14]In practice, we can use forecasts for a number of periods past the end of the sample, which should improve the reliability of the potential output measure toward the end of the sample period.

windows and observation weights. See Scacciavillani and Swagel (1999) for more details and an application of this filter.

The RMS has the advantage of removing the effects of outliers that are not close to the particular smoothed value. It also allows for the possibility of structural change because the window of data that is being smoothed shifts.

Cubic Spline-Smoothing Method (CSSM)

Cubic spline smoothing is popular in curve-fitting applications and for interpolating data (e.g., quarterly data from observed annual data). The cubic spline function partitions the data into N "knots." In this case, the knots are simply periods. The knots may be all the same length or may differ (e.g., at the beginning and/or end of the period). A cubic spline function, $g_i(Z)$, is then defined for ith knot, and each cubic spline function is constrained so that where the knots meet, the function values, slopes, and second derivatives are equal (to ensure a smooth and continuous curve). As in the HP filter, the cubic spline measure of potential output requires the specification of λ, which provides the tradeoff between smoothness and fit. The potential output measure, $g(Z)$ is then derived from the following optimization problem:

$$Min\left[\sum_{t=0}^{T}(y_t - g(Z)_t)^2 + \int_{Z_1}^{Z_N}d^2g(Z)dZ\right]. \quad (5)$$

The choice of λ determines the polynomial order of the general solution. The choice of λ can be determined by the data in a similar way to Coe and McDermott's approach by choosing λ according to the generalized cross-validation (GCV) criteria, which essentially chooses λ to minimize the out-of-sample forecast error on average.[15]

The cubic spline approach is a smoothing methodology which, like the other filtering methods, has the advantage of a minimal data requirement. The knots provide a means to allow for structural breaks and minimize the impact of outliers on the estimate of potential output. The variable knot width allows for the possibility of increasing or decreasing the number of observations in the first and last knots. Thus, reducing the size of the last knot might improve the measure of potential output and the output gap for the most recent period. The spline-smoothing estimator can be interpreted as a variable bandwidth kernel estimator.

Wavelets Filters

The wavelets methodology provides a "de-noising" approach to extracting a series for potential output that does not rely on arbitrary assumption regarding the regularity of fluctuations. Rather, the approach maps the observed data into more general functional spaces, the orthogonal bases of which are called "wavelets." The appendix to Scacciavillani and Swagel (1999) provides an overview of the wavelets theory and a technical discussion of how the filter works, while the main paper provides an application of the wavelets filter to deriving potential output, which is compared with the potential output from a number of other approaches.

Unobservable Components Methods

The unobservable components methods provide a means of estimating unobservable variables, such as NAIRU and potential output, from the observed data on output, inflation, and unemployment. The explicit relationships between the observed and unobserved variables are specified in what is called "state space" form in the measurement or observation equation, which is a general way of representing dynamic systems in which the observed variables are specified in terms of the unobservable variables or state variables. A separate system of equations, the transition equation, specifies the autoregressive processes assumed to generate the state variables. The unobservable variables can then be estimated using what is known as the Kalman filter.[16] The unobservable components model has been developed for a univariate case (decomposing output into a stochastic trend and a cyclical component) and multivariate case (relating inflation, the output gap, and the unemployment gap to derive NAIRU and a measure of potential output). For multivariate applications and further details of the methodology, see Apel and Jansson (1999) and Cerra and Saxena (2000). The latter study discusses extensions, such as the inclusion of common permanent components and the possibility of asymmetric growth rates via the use of a latent Markov-switching state variable.

This method has the very attractive feature of allowing the explicit specification of the relationships between output, inflation, and unemployment, thus providing theory-consistent estimates of potential

---

[15]For a fuller discussion of the use of cubic splines, the data-determined choice of λ, and an empirical application, see Khatri and Solomou (1996).

[16]For a given set of starting values and model parameters, the Kalman filter generates a sequence of optimal conditional predictions of the observable variables. The prediction errors are then used in a maximum likelihood routine to find the optimal set of parameters and corresponding estimates of the unobservable components.

output and the output gap.[17] The requirement of an explicit specification of these relationships, however, means that the measures of potential output and output gap are contingent on this specification.

Also, the method requires explicit assumptions on the form of the data-generating process for the observable variables. For the univariate approach, Quah (1992) has shown that "without additional ad hoc restrictions, those characterizations are completely uninformative for the relative importance of the underlying permanent and transitory components." The multivariate representations have followed, partly in response to this criticism, but they still maintain the assumption that the permanent component of output behaves like a random walk, while in reality the dynamics of output are likely to be much more complex (see Dupasquier, Guay, and St. Amant, 1999). Furthermore, the results of the unobservable components method are often sensitive to the initial "guesses" for the parameters.

Methods Employing Structural Relationships

The Production Function Approach

The production function methodology represents the middle ground between a full-scale structural model and the various univariate approaches, such as filters and unobservable components (De Masi, 1997). The methodology in its simplest form involves the estimation of a production function, most often using the Cobb-Douglas form with two inputs, capital (K) and labor (L), and constant returns to scale. Thus, the production function is specified as:

$$lnY_t = A_t + \alpha lnK + (1 - \alpha)lnL, \qquad (6)$$

where A_t is the level of total factor productivity (TFP) and α and $(1-\alpha)$ are the output share of capital and labor, respectively. The production function can either be estimated (e.g., as a cointegrating equation), or the value of α can be imposed (guided by historical data on capital's or labor's share in output).[18] The level of TFP can be derived residually (Solow's residual) from (6).

To derive potential output from the production function specification, the inputs and TFP have to be set at their trend levels, consistent with full employment and full capacity utilization. Labor input consistent with NAIRU (L^*) could be derived by multiplying the labor force by (1–NAIRU). The trend component of TFP is also required and can be derived in a number of ways, including using smoothing techniques described above.

Extensions to the basic methodology include the refinement of inputs through quality-adjusting capital and labor; the use of more flexible functional forms for specifying the production function; and the explicit modeling of productivity by including technology-determining variables such as research and development, education, and spillovers (see Adams and Coe, 1990).

The production function approach has the attractive feature of determining potential output in a framework that can explicitly account for the contributions of capital, labor, and TFP to output growth. The production function, however, runs into a number of difficult conceptual and data problems, well documented in the literature (see Griliches and Mairesse, 1995, and references therein).

- The most basic criticism stems from the fact that the production function may not be identified because of simultaneity problems.[19]

- The production function specification typically relies on an overly simplistic and probably restrictive representation of the technology.

- The method requires the estimation of NAIRU or some NAIRU-consistent level of labor (L^*). If smoothing techniques are used to derive (L^*) and for the trend TFP growth, then the problems of trend estimation for GDP have shifted to trend estimation of inputs (and TFP).

- Smoothing techniques for L^* and TFP also have the problem of unreliable endpoints, which will thus affect the reliability of production function-based estimates of potential output at endpoints, and, importantly, for the most recent observation.

- The production function approach is considerably more demanding in terms of data than filtering approaches, and the nature of the inputs data—particularly the capital stock calcula-

---

[17]Apel and Jansson (1999) argue that, although most economists would agree that there is a close relationship between the output gap and the unemployment gap and between these gaps and the development of inflation, most studies disregard at least one of these two conditions. They propose a multivariate unobservable component model that includes the first (Okun's law) and the second (Phillips curve) relationship in the estimation of potential output and NAIRU.

[18]If the production function is specified as a cointegrating regression, and output, labor, and capital have unit roots, then the residual-based TFP, if nonstationary, implies that a lack of a cointegrating regression will be obtained if using the Engle-Granger test, and

possibly even if using a system cointegration test (see Scacciavillani and Swagel, 1999). Estimates of α might be obtained from estimating the production function in first differences.

[19]If producers choose inputs to maximize profits after observing output and input prices, then the production function disturbances will feed through into the choice of variable inputs; thus the exogeneity assumption required for estimating the production function will not hold, and OLS estimates will be biased.

tions—implies significant potential for measurement errors in inputs.

- The production function is also likely to suffer from omitted variable bias.

Demand-Side Models

Bayoumi and others (1999) suggest that there are two basic methods of estimating the output gap: demand-side methods, which relate the output gap directly to measures of spare capacity in the economy and supply-side measures, such as the production function approach. Some researchers have combined these methods in simultaneous equation models, such as Adams and Coe (1990) or Blanchard and Quah (1993). Bayoumi estimates demand-side measures of the output gap by using a series of measures of slack in the economy—namely, the unemployment rate, the ratio of job seekers to job offers, capacity utilization rates, a combination of these measures, and an inverted Phillips curve. Measures of potential output and the output gap are derived from regressions of the log of real GDP on the slack variable (or variables) together with a polynomial in the time trend, and regression of a standard Phillips curve, again including polynomial time trend, that is inverted so that output is on the right-hand side of the equation.

The proposed demand-side method is straightforward and intuitively appealing. However, it does not take into account the time series properties of the variables. In particular, as mentioned above, output series tend to be integrated, difference stationary, and not trend stationary. Thus the use of a time trend, whether linear or polynomial, is not an appropriate means to isolate the stochastic permanent component of output (i.e., potential output) or detrend output to derive the output gap. Furthermore, while the output series is likely to be integrated, economic theory would tend to suggest that the series for unemployment, capacity utilization rates, and the vacancy ratio are unlikely to be integrated in the long run. Thus, a simple linear regression may be spurious, in the sense of Granger and Newbold (1974).

Structural Vector Autoregressions (VARs)

The structural VAR approaches that have been employed recently to estimate potential output (see Scacciavillani and Swagel, 1999; Dupasquier, Guay, and St. Amant, 1999; and Cerra and Saxena, 2000) follow from Blanchard and Quah (1993). The general method combines aspects of both the Keynesian and neoclassical traditions in that it associates potential output with aggregate supply and supply shocks, and cyclical/transitory fluctuations with changes in aggregate demand. The Blanchard and Quah method employs a structural VAR in the sense that there are identifying restrictions imposed on the long-run effects of impacts on output and unemployment. These long-run restrictions are used to identify structural supply and demand shocks by allowing supply shocks to have a permanent effect on output, while demand shocks have only a temporary effect on output. The method has been extended, using the same idea of imposing long-run restrictions for the purpose of identification, to multivariate VARs and to the use of alternative variables (see King and others, 1991; Bayoumi and Eichengreen, 1992; Scacciavillani and Swagel, 1999; and Cerra and Saxena, 2000).

The approach is appealing, as it derives an estimate of potential output that employs a clear theoretical basis for the restrictions that identify permanent and transitory shocks. This method has several advantages.

- It is not unduly restrictive in the dynamics imposed on the permanent shocks that affect potential output. Dupasquier, Guay, and St. Amant (1999) compare the structural VAR approach with two alternative multivariate methodologies, namely the Cochrane and multivariate Beveridge-Nelson approaches to deriving potential output, and find that the dynamics of permanent shocks are more complex than the random walk assumed by the other approaches.

- The approach allows the dynamics of permanent shocks to be included in potential output. This is particularly appealing because one perverse implication of defining potential output as a random walk with drift is that, when the immediate effect of a permanent positive shock is smaller than the long-run effect, the output gap (observed output—potential output) is negative until the full effect of the positive shock has fed through.

- The potential output gap measures derived are not subject to end-sample biases or increased uncertainty.

The structural VAR method also has certain disadvantages.

- The approach is limited in its ability to identify different types of shocks (at most, there can be the same number of types as variables used in the VAR).

- In most applications, the method assumes uncorrelated supply and demand shocks. Theory provides numerous instances where shocks have varying demand and supply characteristics (Cerra and Saxena, 2000).[20]

---

[20]For example, a technology shock may affect supply but may simultaneously increase demand through wealth effects.

- Finally, although the approach is not demanding in terms of data, the method is less straightforward to apply than many of the other approaches, as it requires some nontrivial programming.

References

Adams, Charles, and David Coe, 1990, "A Systems Approach to Estimating the Natural Rate of Unemployment and Potential Output for the United States," *Staff Papers*, International Monetary Fund, Vol. 37 (February), pp. 232–93.

Apel, Michael, and Per Jansson, 1999, "A Theory-Consistent System Approach for Estimating Potential Output and the NAIRU," *Economics Letters*, Vol. 64 (September), pp. 271–75.

Bank Negara Malaysia, 1999, *Annual Report* (Kuala Lumpur).

Baxter, Marianne, and Robert G. King, 1995, "Measuring Business Cycles: Approximate Band-Pass Filters for Economic Time Series," NBER Working Paper No. 5022 (Cambridge, Massachusetts: National Bureau of Economic Research).

Bayoumi, Tamim, and Barry Eichengreen, 1992, "Is There a Conflict Between EC Enlargement and European Monetary Unification?" NBER Working Paper No. 3950 (Cambridge, Massachusetts: National Bureau of Economic Research).

Bayoumi, Tamim, and others, 1999, *Japan—Selected Issues* (Washington: International Monetary Fund).

Blanchard, Olivier, and Danny Quah, 1993, "The Dynamic Effects of Aggregate Demand and Supply Disturbances," *American Economic Review*, Vol. 83 (June), pp. 653–58.

Cerra, Valerie, and Sweta C. Saxena, 2000, "Alternative Methods of Estimating Potential Output and the Output Gap: An Application to Sweden," IMF Working Paper 00/59 (Washington: International Monetary Fund).

Charemza, Wojciech W., and Derek F. Deadman, 1992, *New Directions in Econometric Practice: General to Specific Modeling, Cointegration and Vector Autoregression* (Brookfield, Vermont: Edward Elgar).

Chhibber, Ajay, and others, 1989, "Inflation, Price Controls, and Fiscal Adjustment in Zimbabwe," World Bank Policy, Planning, and Research Working Paper No. 192 (Washington: World Bank).

Coe, David, and John McDermott, 1997, "Does the Gap Model Work in Asia?" *Staff Papers*, International Monetary Fund, Vol. 44 (March), pp. 59–80.

Cogley, Timothy, and James Nason, 1995, "Effects of the Hodrick-Prescott Filter on Trend and Difference Stationary Time Series: Implications for Business Cycle Research," *Journal of Economic Dynamics and Control*, Vol. 19 (January–February), pp. 253–78.

de Brouwer, Gordon, and Neil Ericsson, 1998, "Modeling Inflation in Australia," *Journal of Business and Economic Statistics*, Vol. 16 (October), pp. 433–49.

De Masi, Paula, 1997, "IMF Estimates of Output: Theory and Practice," IMF Working Paper 97/177 (Washington: International Monetary Fund).

Dupasquier, Chantal, Alain Guay, and Pierre St. Amant, 1999, "A Survey of Alternative Methodologies for Estimating Potential Output and the Output Gap," *Journal of Macroeconomics*, Vol. 21, pp. 577–95.

Granger, Clive, and Paul Newbold, 1974, "Spurious Regressions in Econometrics," *Journal of Econometrics*, Vol. 2 (July), pp. 111–20.

Griliches, Zvi, and Jacques Mairesse, 1995, "Production Functions: The Search for Identification," NBER Working Paper No. 5067 (Cambridge, Massachusetts: National Bureau of Economic Research).

Guay, Alain, and Pierre St. Amant, 1996, "Do Mechanical Filters Provide a Good Approximation of Business Cycles?" Technical Report No. 78 (Ottawa: Bank of Canada).

Härdle, Wolfgang, 1990, *Applied Nonparametric Regression* (New York: Cambridge University Press).

Harvey, Andrew C., and Albert Jaeger, 1993, "Detrending, Stylized Facts and the Business Cycle," *Journal of Applied Econometrics*, Vol. 8 (July–September), pp. 231–47.

Hodrick, Robert J., and Edward C. Prescott, 1997, "Postwar U.S. Business Cycles: An Empirical Investigation," *Journal of Money, Credit, and Banking*, Vol. 29 (February), pp. 1–16.

Jonsson Gunnar, 1999, "Inflation, Money Demand, and Purchasing Power Parity in South Africa," IMF Working Paper 99/122 (Washington: International Monetary Fund).

Khatri, Yongesh, and Solomons Solomou, 1996, "Climate and Fluctuations in Agricultural Output, 1867–1913," University of Cambridge, DAE Working Paper No. 9617 (Cambridge, Massachusetts).

King, Robert, and others, 1991, "Stochastic Trends and Economic Fluctuations," *American Economic Review*, Vol. 81 (September), pp. 819–40.

Lim, Cheng H., and Laura Papi, 1997, "An Econometric Analysis of the Determinants of Inflation in Turkey," IMF Working Paper 97/170 (Washington: International Monetary Fund).

Nelson, Charles, and Charles Plosser, 1982, "Trends and Random Walks in Macroeconomic Time Series: Some Evidence and Implications," *Journal of Monetary Economics*, Vol. 10 (September), pp. 139–62.

Quah, Danny, 1992, "The Relative Importance of Permanent and Transitory Components: Identification and Some Theoretical Bounds," *Econometrica*, Vol. 60 (January), pp. 107–18.

Razzak, Weshah, 1995, "The Inflation-Output Trade-Off: Is the Phillips Curve Symmetric? Evidence from New Zealand," Reserve Bank of New Zealand Discussion Paper G95/7 (January), pp. 1–17.

Scacciavillani, Fabio, and Phillip Swagel, 1999, "Measures of Potential Output: An Application to Israel," IMF Working Paper 99/96 (Washington: International Monetary Fund).

Söderlind, Paul, 1994, "Cyclical Properties of a Real Business Cycle Model," *Journal of Applied Econometrics*, Vol. 9 (December), pp.113–22.

Stock, James, and Mark Watson, 1999, "Forecasting Inflation," *Journal of Monetary Economics*, Vol. 44 (October), pp. 293–335.

IV   Challenges to Fiscal Management

Olin Liu

A lesson from the Asian crisis is that the effectiveness of Malaysia's fiscal policy in demand management may benefit from greater flexibility. While Malaysia's tradition of fiscal prudence provided a buffer against adverse shocks during the crisis, structural rigidities in public finances rendered fiscal policy less responsive to the changing economic environment. A key challenge to fiscal management is to make it flexible enough to function as an effective countercyclical tool within the framework dedicated to maintaining long-term fiscal sustainability.

Remedies for improving fiscal flexibility could include extension of the fiscal planning horizon to cover the course of the business cycle, to be supported by well-defined safeguards and escape clauses (for fiscal rules); more realistic economic forecasts and revenue projections as the basis for setting fiscal targets; a structural fiscal balance concept; and greater use of automatic stabilizers and contingency measures in the budget.

Introduction and Recent Developments

During the 1980s, Malaysia experienced large fiscal deficits and high public debt-to-GDP ratios. Fiscal consolidation, begun in the mid-1980s, aimed at reducing imbalances with the support of strong government commitment to a rule-based fiscal policy, privatization, and reorientation of capital spending to basic infrastructure development and other productive sectors. During the period of fiscal consolidation (1992–97), fiscal policy was geared more toward achieving the medium-term development objectives and was used, to a lesser extent, as a tool for demand management (Figure 4.1).

Public programs were formulated within the framework of five-year development plans aimed at promoting economic growth over the medium term through capacity expansion; improvements in productivity; and adequate provision of public infrastructure, utilities, and other modern services. The

government played an important role in mobilizing public and private resources to finance its development programs, including through off-budget and quasi-fiscal activities. In support of the development strategy, fiscal consolidation was conducted mainly through the tightening of the operating budget that led to current surpluses, which in turn helped to moderate overheating pressures on the economy arising from accelerated money and credit growth, together with a surge in capital inflows.

In the context of the consolidation, Malaysia's fiscal conservatism was reflected in the rule of disallowing an "operating deficit" in the annual budget to help strengthen the financial position of the federal government. While revenue performance determined the level of recurrent spending, the capacity to raise nonbank financing determined the size of capital spending, thereby minimizing budgetary financing from the banking system. This rule, together with a tradition of conservative revenue projections,

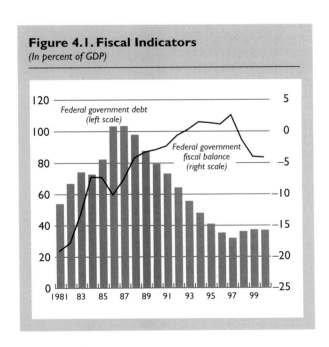

Figure 4.1. Fiscal Indicators
(In percent of GDP)

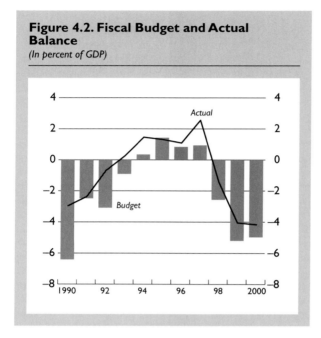

Figure 4.2. Fiscal Budget and Actual Balance
(In percent of GDP)

led to large operating—and overall—surpluses each year during 1990–97 (Figure 4.2). The strengthened fiscal position served the country well during the ensuing crisis, in that it provided substantial scope for a countercyclical fiscal policy and funding for financial sector restructuring.

At the outset of the crisis, Malaysia tightened macroeconomic policies to reduce vulnerability. The policy stance, together with a preemptive reform of the financial sector, was intended to help contain inflation and the current account deficit, reduce credit growth, and dampen the pressure on domestic demand. It was also expected to instill salutary effects on finances and market confidence. Eventually, the 1998 budget was revised to reflect a rebalancing of policies toward a smaller surplus.[1] In anticipation of declining revenue in line with an economic downturn, the surplus was to result from lower current outlays and deferred infrastructure projects. These measures were also expected to help reduce imports and contain the high leverage of corporations.

Notwithstanding these policy initiatives, market confidence faltered markedly against broader adverse developments in the region, including concerns about financial system vulnerability. Economic activities also slowed much faster than anticipated, which proved to be a significant factor that further damp-

ened market confidence. Against this background, the government readjusted its policy mix toward an expansionary policy and has maintained an expansionary stance since mid-1998 aimed at reactivating economic growth and, thereby, ensuring socioeconomic stability. A fiscal stimulus package was introduced that included a social safety net to mitigate the effects of economic adjustment on the most vulnerable groups, as well as large increases in capital spending, especially for infrastructure and other social sector projects.

The countercyclical fiscal policy has been delivered largely through discretionary measures. The fiscal stimulus package of 1998–2001 focused on selected capital projects designed to ensure maximum effect on economic growth, minimum leakage to imports, large export potential, and a short gestation period in terms of providing value-added to the economy. Large projects were restructured into smaller segments to facilitate financing. Beyond the budget, the government also provided fiscal impulse through off-budget operations, facilitated by the quasi-fiscal institutions. Existing credit schemes were expanded, and new specialized funds were set up to ensure continued access to credit at reasonable cost for priority sectors and projects.

The impact of the expansionary fiscal policy was initially weaker than expected and came with a significant lag (1998–99). Spending cuts implemented earlier could not be reversed easily. The fiscal rule of disallowing an operating deficit also limited the scope of using fiscal policy as a tool for demand management. In 1998 and 1999, the fiscal impulse, estimated at about 2 percent and 3 percent of GDP, respectively, was well below the budget targets (by 2 percent and 1 percent of GDP, respectively), which explained in part the slow turnaround in domestic demand (Box 4.1). Fiscal stimulus was enhanced in 2000 through both revenue and expenditure measures. The budget deficit of 4.3 percent of GDP, and possibly the lagged effects from projects initiated under previous years' budgets, provided a strong impetus to the recovery in domestic demand.

Despite the larger fiscal deficit of the government, the overall financial position of the public sector was contained by the strengthened balance sheets of the nonfinancial public enterprises and benefited largely from banking and corporate restructuring, a significant turnaround in economic activities, and high oil prices.

A key challenge is to ensure that fiscal policy in Malaysia can contribute to effective demand management. This would require greater flexibility in fiscal policy to respond to domestic and external macroeconomic shocks in an appropriate and timely way, while maintaining fiscal prudence to

---

[1]This degree of fiscal easing, which was supported by the IMF, turned out to be insufficient.

Box 4.1. Fiscal Policy in Malaysia, 1997–2000

Following the initial stage of tighter fiscal policy at the outset of the crisis, the government rebalanced its approach through policy easing in response to a sharp decline in domestic demand that became evident by mid-1998. Targeted budget surpluses were reduced, some previously announced cuts in social expenditures were reinstated, and additional capital spending was implemented. Off-budget spending, most notably through privatized infrastructure projects, also provided additional fiscal impetus.

However, the countercyclical fiscal policy was adopted later in Malaysia than in other Asian crisis countries. Fiscal policies, which had been contractionary at the eve of the crisis, were eased in Korea and Thailand and subsequently shifted to expansionary stances in late 1997 (in Thailand) and early 1998 (in Korea). In Malaysia, by contrast, the fiscal stance remained significantly contractionary throughout most of 1997 (i.e., a negative fiscal impulse of 1.3 percent of GDP); this was consistent with the advice of the IMF at that time. The shift in fiscal policy took place in mid-1998. Even then, the actual fiscal impulse was smaller than the budgetary target (by about 2 percent of GDP on average during 1998–99), owing in part to traditionally conservative revenue projections in the budget and insufficient flexibility in fiscal management (see figure, below).

Fiscal policy in Malaysia shifted to an expansionary stance in 1999 in support of economic recovery. The fiscal stimulus provided through the budget and off-budget operations helped to offset in part a continued decline in private demand. The fiscal impulse, including off-budget stimulus and estimated at about 3½ percent of GDP, was less than the budget target of 4¼ percent of GDP and was backloaded to the second half of the year. On a cumulative basis, the fiscal impulse in Malaysia during 1997–99 became larger than in the other Asian crisis countries (see figure, below).[1]

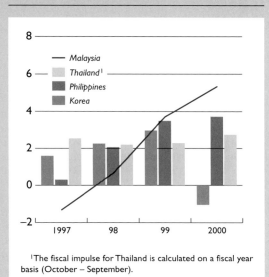

Cumulative Fiscal Impulse of Selected Asian Countries
(In percent of GDP)

[1]The fiscal impulse for Thailand is calculated on a fiscal year basis (October – September).

Still, the recovery in domestic demand in Malaysia remained weak in 1999, which prompted another fiscal stimulus in 2000. The budget deficit reached 4.3 percent of GDP. The economy responded with an impressive real growth of 8½ percent. Domestic demand also mounted a strong recovery, growing by more than 15 percent.

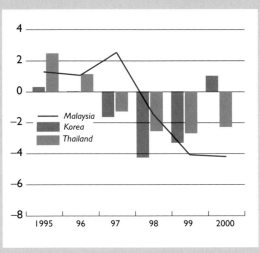

Overall Fiscal Balances of Selected Asian Countries
(In percent of GDP)

[1]In general, the fiscal impulse is used for analyzing the fiscal stance under a stable economic environment; therefore, this information should be interpreted with care.

ensure medium-term fiscal sustainability and growth prospects. The remainder of this section reviews policy options that would provide such flexi-bility in the context of a medium-term fiscal strategy, and that explores operational guidelines to improve policy effectiveness.

Fiscal Policy Rules and Recent Experience

Malaysia follows an explicit fiscal policy rule that disallows an operating deficit in any given year. This rule aims at making a credible commitment to long-term fiscal sustainability by applying discipline to annual budgets. Other fiscal rules that have a longer time horizon are also at work and are predetermined in the medium-term framework of Malaysia's five-year development plan to ensure broad consistency with the rule on the operating balance. These are

- a balanced budget rule under the seventh five-year development plan (1996–2000), revised in mid-1998 in the context of the fiscal stimulus plan, that targets an overall federal government deficit of no more than 6 percent of GNP by the end of the plan period;

- a spending rule that places an aggregate ceiling on capital expenditure during the seventh five-year plan period; and

- a borrowing rule that sets a ceiling on the total outstanding stock of federal government debt during the seventh five-year plan, with a subceiling on external federal debt.

Overall, the rules are well defined as to the target variables and compliance criteria, which are approved by the parliament and are broadly enforceable. Internal consistencies of the fiscal rules with other macroeconomic policies—such as low inflation, sustainable government debt, and noninflationary financing—are safeguarded by the medium-term policy framework. Compliance with fiscal rules is enforced mostly through administrative means, although deviation from the rules requires parliamentary approval. There is no financial penalty for nonobservance. Nevertheless, a violation of the rules could entail loss of credibility of the government in the eyes of parliament and financial markets, as well as the public.

Notwithstanding fiscal discipline, the rules preclude the use of cyclical indicators and escape clauses, thereby constraining fiscal policy from becoming an effective countercyclical tool. Furthermore, the rules are assessed against fiscal targets that do not cover off-budget and quasi-fiscal operations, which lead to nontransparency in accounting and fiscal forecasting, as well as difficulty in assessing the total impact of fiscal policy and in estimating future government obligations.

While effective in imposing fiscal discipline, these rules have proved to be procyclical during the recent economic downturn. Conservative forecasting of tax revenues constrains the effectiveness of fiscal planning. Capital spending on projects tends to rely on discretionary measures, which can exert pressure on the implementation capacity. Procedural bottlenecks, insufficient financing, and long implementation periods for new projects also reduce the timeliness of the intended fiscal impact.

The government has made various adjustments to overcome these constraints during the course of the crisis. Monitoring of both revenue and expenditure in particular was stepped up through monthly meetings of the high-level Cash Flow Committee. In order to speed up spending, ministries were given the flexibility to move funds within the same economic categories. Contingency reserves were used for capital spending with the approval of the finance minister. The midterm review of the seventh five-year development plan (completed in mid-1998) was particularly timely in redirecting fiscal policy toward stimulating the economy in the wake of a sharp contraction.

The government also used off-budget operations and quasi-fiscal activities to reinforce the fiscal impetus. A specialized fund was established to provide financing to "privatized" infrastructure projects. During 1997–99, a total of 16 large projects (mostly for infrastructure development) were selected by the government for implementation through the Malaysia Infrastructure Development Bank. Additional loans were obtained mostly from quasi-government entities and bilateral external borrowing (under the Miyazawa initiative) with explicit guarantees from the government (Appendix I).

Enhancing Fiscal Policy Responsiveness to Business Cycles

Fiscal policy can be effective and countercyclical if the rules are so designed and institutional arrangements are in place to enforce them. The key issue in designing fiscal rules is the balance between the short-term need for growth and employment and the long-term desire for fiscal sustainability. To achieve an appropriate balance, flexibility is critical in the formulation and application of these rules, while clearly defined guidelines and escape clauses will safeguard the credibility of the authorities in pursuing fiscal prudence over the medium term.

Formulation of Fiscal Rules

Flexibility can be incorporated into fiscal rules by the following methods:

- Expanding the horizon for budget formulation, including the application of fiscal rules, to cover the course of a business cycle would provide the economy with improved shock-absorptive capacity. For instance, the fiscal rule on the annual operating budget could be modified to allow an operating deficit during an economic downturn while observing the balance (on average) over the course of a business cycle. This would require a medium-term fiscal framework for planning, analysis, and forecasting (Box 4.2).

- Setting fiscal targets on the basis of a structural balance concept would allow revenue and expenditure to adjust automatically for deviations in output. Given the authorities' commitment to fiscal consolidation over the medium term, there is merit to considering the use of the aggregate budget deficit as a target variable, supplemented by a subceiling on the operating budget. The pace of fiscal consolidation should follow a carefully mapped convergence plan to a structural balance.

- Enhancing the role of built-in stabilizers would help to strengthen the countercyclical influence of fiscal policy while limiting the use of discretionary measures.[2] More realistic revenue projections can also facilitate assessment of the effects of built-in stabilizers. On the expenditure side, the introduction of a well-targeted social safety net and provision of unemployment benefits could greatly improve the responsiveness of fiscal policy.

- Establishing safeguards and escape clauses would allow fiscal policy to respond to large unforeseen shocks. The choices of cyclical indicators and conditions that would invoke the escape clauses need to be defined in advance and as precisely as possible. The criteria should be transparent so that the timing for triggering the escape clauses are known to the public. Choices of cyclical indicators should be sensitive to the business cycle (such as the level of private investment) and should be able to be monitored. To be effective, the coverage of the budget should include all off-budget and quasi-fiscal operations.

- Introducing contingency measures during the budget process, either to add stimulus or withdraw it as required, could include the elimination (or imposition) of a surtax and introduction of a stabilization fund. An across-the-board increase (or cut) in capital spending, although effective, should be used only as a last resort. These and other measures, specified in advance, can be triggered during budget execution if actual budget performance deviates significantly from the planned path.

Greater Flexibility in Fiscal Policy Management

Fiscal consolidation over the medium term will require a shift from fiscal stimulus to a significant scaling back of development expenditure. It is a challenge to withdraw the stimulus without major disruption to economic activities. Capacity for policy analysis and forecasting will need to be strengthened, taking into consideration the linkages between fiscal and monetary policies, desired rate of growth, inflation, and other macroeconomic variables that influence budget preparation and execution. Shifting gears with minimal disruption to the economy could involve several initiatives.

- Developing a medium-term fiscal framework as an integral part of the macroeconomic framework. This fiscal framework should include an analysis of the budget sensitivity to exogenous shocks and help identify major fiscal vulnerabilities. It should also incorporate forward-looking estimates on resource constraints based on actual and projected macroeconomic variables. Cyclical indicators should be identified to reflect business cycle behavior. Contingency measures (e.g., increases in current and capital expenditures or tax measures) could be formulated in the context of this medium-term framework, which would be regularly updated and applied on an annual rolling basis.

- Assessing the fiscal policy stance based on consolidated public accounts. Provision of fully consolidated details of off-budget and quasi-fiscal activities for both revenue and expenditures would greatly enhance transparency and allow the full impact of fiscal policy to be analyzed. The netting of certain expenditures should be replaced by transactions on a gross basis.

- Improving the quality and reliability of revenue forecasts by adopting a more systematic, model-based approach. A simple structural model can be developed to cover as many different components of revenue as feasible, particularly the major taxes. In this connection, there are two basic forecasting methods: the effective tax rate method and the revenue elasticity method. Time series on various taxes, particularly income taxes for individuals and corporations, need to be updated with a view to developing a microsimulation model for income tax forecasting purposes.

---

[2]Although Malaysia recently took measures to enhance the stabilizers on the revenue side by shifting to current year income tax assessment, stabilizers on the expenditure side remain absent.

Box 4.2. Fiscal Policy Responses to the Business Cycle

There are two schools of thought. In line with the Keynesian theory, one group argues that the formulation of fiscal policy should be responsive and countercyclical. Hence, one would observe a positive correlation between tax revenues and output, but a negative correlation between government spending and output. During an economic slowdown, the government should lower taxes and increase spending to stimulate the economy. The counterargument inspired by Barro (1979), however, says that fiscal policy should be neutral over the business cycle and respond only to unanticipated shocks that affect the government's budget constraint.

A study by Vegh and Talvi (2000) finds that fiscal policy in Malaysia follows neither the countercyclical nor the neutral-response views. In fact, based on a sample of 56 countries (1977–94), the study shows that in developing countries (including Malaysia) government spending and taxes are highly procyclical. The authors consider this as the outcome of the variability of the tax base. They find that the tax base fluctuations along with the business cycle are much larger in developing countries than in the G-7 countries. This would imply that, if the Barro prescription were followed, full tax smoothing would result in large budget surpluses in a boom and large budget deficits in a bust. Vegh and Talvi argue, however, that the political economy could make it costly to run large fiscal surpluses, owing to the pressure to increase public spending in particular on government consumption and nonproductive investments. Thus, developing countries may choose procyclical fiscal policy as their optimal fiscal response to favorable shocks in their tax base. Their argument is in contrast with the standard explanation for procyclical fiscal policy in developing countries that builds on the imperfect access to international credit markets during unfavorable times. They suggest that it is the inability of the government to generate large enough surpluses during expansion that forces it to borrow less during recession (see figure, upper right-hand side).

The study suggested that in Malaysia the budget revenue, government consumption, and private consumption are procyclical.[1] Their correlation coefficients with output are estimated at 0.64, 0.54, and 0.77, respectively (corresponding averages for the Asian crisis countries were 0.66, 0.56, and 0.62, respectively). The procyclical nature of fiscal policy is also found in other developing countries in the sample, although the degrees of correlation are nonhomogenous. Evidence shows that in Malaysia economic expansion during 1991–97 led to real increases in government revenue, but these grew at slower paces than real GDP. Higher revenue exerted pressure for larger government spending. To minimize such pressure, the government developed a tendency to underestimate revenues in the budget. The procyclical nature of the fiscal policy was reversed in 1998–99 through the provision of ad hoc countercyclical fiscal stimulus (see figure, lower right-hand side).

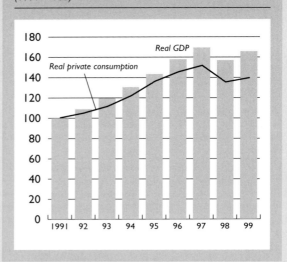

Real GDP and Real Private Consumption
(1991 = 100)

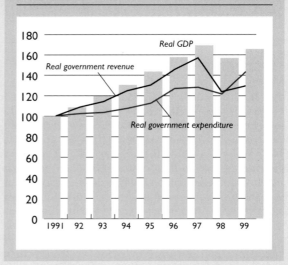

Real GDP and Real Government Revenue
(1991 = 100)

---

[1]Estimation is based on real output with the cyclical components in budget revenue, government consumption, and private consumption (all in real terms).

- Adopting a forward-looking approach to fiscal management by incorporating fiscal monitoring with forecasting. This would help identify possible deviations in fiscal policy stance from the intended path. Tax and expenditure policy options should be reviewed and updated on a timely basis, excluding windfall revenues and nonrecurring expenditures, while taking into account medium-term macroeconomic constraints. It would also be helpful to initiate procedures to review regularly the sources of errors between actual outcome and the quarterly forecast for major budgetary components. Errors could then be analyzed against possible attributes to changes in policies, revisions in macroeconomic assumptions, and/or technical pitfalls in the forecasting model.

- Developing mechanisms for identifying the most and least efficient and effective spending programs, based on economic and social criteria. Results could be disseminated to line ministries as potential candidates for expenditure adjustments. In this connection, high value-added and quick-yielding programs might be identified and targeted according to expenditure policy priorities; this is particularly important where there is a need for additional spending.

- Allowing expenditure switching among sectors or ministries, such as increases in social sector expenditure or public maintenance, together with reductions in less productive spending. Avoiding across-the-board increases (or reductions) as much as possible will limit adverse economic and social impact and the loss of efficiency. Contingent reserves may also be used, with the amount adjusted on an annual rolling basis, to serve as a buffer against unexpected shocks in the future.

Conclusions

Experience in recent years suggests that greater flexibility in fiscal management will help reduce the economic and social costs of a crisis through timely adjustments. This flexibility must be guided by well-defined fiscal rules that aim at enhancing the countercyclical nature of fiscal policy. Specifically, greater flexibility can be achieved through a rules-based framework, with the horizon extended to the medium term. This framework should have a well-defined fiscal target (i.e., a structurally adjusted balance). Temporary deviations from the target will be permitted, however, under clearly defined guidelines to accommodate unforeseen adverse shocks. Political support is critical, as well as institutional arrangements for

budget implementation. Fiscal flexibility would also be enhanced by the effective use of safeguards and escape clauses, realistic revenue projections, and a greater role for automatic stabilizers and contingency measures.

Fiscal flexibility needs to go hand-in-hand with greater transparency. This can be achieved by requiring the government to be explicit about its objectives, ensuring thereby that short-term fiscal policies are consistent with long-term macroeconomic goals. Greater flexibility and transparency will require timely updating of forecasts that highlight the changes in external and domestic conditions. Consolidation of off-budget and quasi-fiscal operations are also important.

Appendix I. Off-Budget and Quasi-Fiscal Operations

For the past few years, the Malaysian government has influenced overall public sector finances through off-budget and quasi-fiscal operations. These activities are often carried out by semi-government entities and other public financial institutions. The framework for these activities has developed as a result of significant government involvement in the past that was essential for achieving the social objectives of rebalancing the ownership structure of the economy. The nature of off-budget and quasi-fiscal operations in Malaysia is mostly related to the government's role, including that of Bank Negara Malaysia, as planner of the economy and regulator of the financial system. The government entrusts the central bank and other semi-government institutions to provide loans for strategic investment plans and to finance large infrastructure projects, financial and corporate sector restructuring, and operations of the informal social safety net.

Despite their potentially significant macroeconomic and financial impact, as well as allocative effects on the economy, off-budget and quasi-fiscal operations are currently outside the consolidated fiscal accounts of the public sector. Contingent liabilities associated with these operations are nonetheless moderate, based on identified information.

Major off-budget and quasi-fiscal operations in Malaysia include the following:[3]

- provision of concessional lending for privatized infrastructure projects through the operation of the Infrastructure Development Fund, a fund es-

---

[3]In addition, the government's contingent liabilities arise from the provision of bank deposit guarantees, which were made explicit in January 1998.

tablished in 1998 to provide off-budget fiscal stimulus through the implementation of large infrastructure projects;

- activities of Khazanah—an entity initially created with the capital from privatization proceeds of public enterprises—that acts as an investment arm of the government for strategic development projects and other activities of national interest;[4]

- financial restructuring of banks, which commenced in 1998, through the operations of Danaharta (to acquire nonperforming loans) and Danamodal (to recapitalize banks);

- provision of explicit government guarantees of loans extended by the Employees' Provident Fund, a public pension fund, and various state-owned trust funds to nonfinancial public enterprises and some privatized projects; bonds issued by Khazanah (up to RM 10 billion); and obligations of Danaharta;

- provision of explicit government guarantees of external loans undertaken by major nonfinancial public enterprises that involve large projects of national interest, and other bilateral and multilateral external loans to public entities, including the state-owned financial institutions (e.g., Malaysia Infrastructure Development Bank);

- extension of subsidized loans by Bank Negara Malaysia for the operation of the informal social safety net, including low-cost housing; and

- potential government burden sharing in resolving the financial troubles of certain privatized projects as well as other quasi-fiscal operations associated with the activities of financial public enterprises.

Among the above-mentioned operations, financial information is mostly available on (i) the operations of Danaharta and Danamodal; (ii) explicit government guarantees of the external loans of major nonfinancial public enterprises undertaking large national projects; (iii) explicit government guarantees of domestic loans extended by the Employees' Provident Fund (and other trust funds) to major nonfinancial public enterprises; and (iv) Bank Negara Malaysia operations associated with the informal social safety net. Information related to the operations of Infrastructure Development Fund and Khazanah, however, is partial, and information of implicit gov-

ernment guarantees, and thus implicit contingent government liability related to certain privatized projects, is very limited.

Privatized Infrastructure Projects

Most off-budget operations were associated with the implementation of large privatized infrastructure projects. Sixty-eight such projects were implemented during 1996–98, with a total cost of RM 67 billion. Financial support from the federal government in terms of advances for land and loans was provided for major infrastructure projects.[5] Initial seed capital was provided from the budget for these projects to help secure long-term commercial loans at favorable terms,[6] with the objectives of improving operating efficiency, saving budgetary resources, reducing administrative burden, and promoting private sector participation in the economy. These projects involved mainly the construction of highways, mass-transit systems, sewage systems, and other utilities for social sector development.

The Infrastructure Development Fund was established in 1998 and was aimed at assisting with the financing of those privatized infrastructure projects whose implementation was significantly delayed in the aftermath of the crisis. The Infrastructure Development Fund had an initial capital of RM 1 billion and is managed by the Malaysia Infrastructure Development Bank. The government provided explicit guarantees for both domestic and external loans undertaken by the Malaysia Infrastructure Development Bank, which amounted to nearly RM 6 billion in 1999. Most of these loans are from the Employees' Provident Fund (RM 4.5 billion) and bilateral sources (RM 1.3 million, under the Miyazawa initiative).

Off-budget capital spending was stepped up in 1999 to provide additional fiscal stimulus to the economy. The government handpicked 16 major projects (mainly in infrastructure, utilities, and social services), amounting to about RM 9 billion (3 percent of GDP), to be financed by the Malaysia Infrastructure Development Bank as part of the off-budget fiscal stimulus. Two-thirds have been finalized, and about RM 1 billion is expected to be disbursed annually during 1999–2001.

More recently, some of these large projects are facing financial difficulties that may have implica-

---

[4]As of end-1999, Khazanah's portfolio included its interests in Tenaga (36 percent of equity); Telekom Malaysia (37 percent); Malaysia Airports Holdings Bhd. (23 percent); and Putrajaya Holdings Sdn. Bhd. (40 percent).

---

[5]Most of the new and major projects were privatized through the build-operate-transfer method.

[6]Interest rates were in the range of 6–8 percent with an average grace period of 6 years and a repayment period of 15–18 years. These are in line with the terms of the government loans for these projects.

Table 4.1. Quasi-Fiscal Contingent Liabilities
(Outstanding stock at end of period, in percent of GDP)

	1997	1998	1999
Federal government guaranteed loans	8.3	11.6	16.8
Domestic	5.0	7.1	8.3
Foreign	3.2	3.4	3.7
Additional identified debt guaranteed by the government[1]	0.1	1.1	4.8
Guaranteed loans for the Malaysia Infrastructure Development Bank	0.1	0.2	0.5
Guaranteed loans for Danaharta and Permodalan Nasional Bhd.	...	0.9	3.6
Guaranteed loans for Petroliam Nasional Bhd.	...	...	0.7

Sources: Data provided by the Malaysian authorities; and IMF staff estimates.
[1]Excluding Danamodal bond issue of RM 7.7 billion (about 2½ percent of GDP) as of February 15, 2000.

tions to the budget. The issue has caught the attention of the public, who has questioned the viability of these projects, as well as the governance issue related to government subsidies (both explicit or implicit) in the form of budget spending or soft loans.

There are no explicit government guarantees associated with these projects. Given the nature of these projects, however, the government has indicated that it may consider some form of financial support, depending on the merit of each case. Modalities could include a third-party takeover, buy back at discounts, and/or a rescue operation through cash injection. In the event of a government takeover, outstanding loans of the government would be automatically converted to equity holding in the project. Liquidation is not likely, as these projects involve national infrastructure and social services. The manner in which the government handles these projects, including the extent to which best practices are followed, is likely to have significant implications for public finances and development programs in the future.

The government is working on improving the framework within which privatized projects are regulated particularly with respect to operating standards and quality of services, to ensure adherence to terms and conditions stipulated in the privatization agreements. One proposal is to establish sectoral regulatory bodies, initially to cover energy and gas, transportation, telecommunications, and water supply and sewerage systems. Under such a framework, the emphasis will be on penalties for noncompliance with the terms and conditions of the agreements.

Contingent Liabilities of the Government

Provisions of explicit guarantees to off-budget capital spending and operations of Danaharta have raised government contingent liabilities[7] in recent years. Although data on these activities are not systematically reported in a consolidated manner, some information has been identified (Table 4.1).

Appendix II. Fiscal Measurement: Methodology Note

Definition of Cyclically Neutral Balance, Fiscal Stance, and Fiscal Impulse

Cyclically neutral balance measures the fiscal position relative to a base year; it is defined as the difference between the cyclically neutral revenue and expenditure. Cyclically neutral revenue represents a constant revenue-to-nominal-GDP ratio, while cyclically neutral expenditure represents a constant expenditure-to-potential-GDP ratio (excluding unemployment benefits), both relative to the base year.

Fiscal stance measures the difference between the actual balance and the cyclically neutral balance. A positive fiscal stance (i.e., a situation where the actual deficit is larger than the cyclically neutral deficit) indicates that fiscal policy is adding stimulus to the economy.

---

[7]Information on contingent liabilities of the government associated with the provision of implicit guarantees is yet to be compiled and consolidated.

Fiscal impulse is defined as the change in the fiscal stance; it provides a sense of direction and the magnitude of the new fiscal stimulus to the economy. While the fiscal stance depends critically on the neutral balance and, thus, the selection of the base year, the fiscal impulse is not sensitive to this problem, which makes it a more useful indicator than the fiscal stance.

Calculation of Cyclically Neutral Balance, Fiscal Stance, and Fiscal Impulse

- Selecting the base year t_0; $R(t_0) - E(t_0)$ is the cyclically neutral balance in year t_0;
where $R(t_0)$ = cyclically neutral revenue in year t_0; $E(t_0)$ = cyclically neutral expenditure in year t_0.

- Calculating the cyclically neutral revenue for current year t:

$$Neutral\ Revenue = Y(t)^*r,$$

where $Y(t)$ = nominal GDP in year t; r = the GDP share of revenue in the base year t_0.

- Calculating the cyclically neutral expenditure for current year t:

$$Neutral\ Expenditure = \frac{P(t)^*\ AE(t_0) - UB(t_0)}{Y(t_0)},$$

where $P(t)$ = potential nominal GDP in year t; $Y(t_0)$ = nominal GDP in year t_0; $AE(t_0)$ = actual expenditure in t_0; $UB(t_0)$ = unemployment benefit in t_0.

- Calculating the fiscal stance, $S(t)$, in year t:

$$S(t) = [R(t_0) - E(t_0)] - [rY(t) - eP(t)],$$

where $R(t_0) - E(t_0)$ = the cyclically neutral balance in year t_0; $rY(t) - eP(t)$ = the cyclically neutral balance in year t; e = the GDP share of expenditure in the base year t_0.

- Calculating the fiscal impulse, $I(t)$, in year t:

$$I(t) = [S(t)/Y(t)] - [S(t-1)/Y(t-1)].$$

Definition of Structural Fiscal Balance

Structural fiscal balance is the difference between the structural revenue and structural expenditure. The *structural revenue* measures the actual revenue adjusted for the lagged impact in closing the output gap. The *structural expenditure* measures the actual expenditure adjusted for the provision of unemployment benefits for cyclical unemployment (rather than the structural unemployment).

Calculation of Structural Fiscal Balance

- Calculating the structural revenue, $SR(t)$, in year t:

$$SR(t) = \frac{AR(t)^*\ (Output\ Gap)_t^{\alpha}}{(Output\ Gap)_{t-1}^{\beta}},$$

where $AR(t)$ = actual revenue in year t; Output gap = (potential output)/(actual output); α = revenue elasticity (weighted average) in time t; β = revenue elasticity (weighted average) in time $t-1$.

- Calculating the structural expenditure, $SE(t)$, in year t:

$$SE(t) = AE(t) - UB(t)^* \left[\frac{1 - Structural\ Unemployment(t)}{Actual\ Unemployment} \right],$$

where $AE(t)$ = actual expenditure in year t; $UB(t)$ = unemployment benefits in year t.

- Calculating the structural balance, $SB(t)$, in year t:

$$SB(t) = SR(t) - SE(t).$$

The structural balance is often measured in terms of potential GDP.

References

Alesina, Alberto, and Tamim Bayoumi, 1996, "The Costs and Benefits of Fiscal Rules: Evidence from U.S. States," NBER Working Paper No. 5614 (Cambridge, Massachusetts: National Bureau of Economic Research).

Backus, David, Patrick Kehoe, and Finn Kydland, 1995, "International Business Cycles: Theory and Evidence," in *Frontiers of Business Cycle Research*, ed. by Thomas F. Cooley (Princeton, New Jersey: Princeton University Press).

Bank Negara Malaysia, *Annual Report 1999* (Kuala Lumpur).

Barro, Robert, 1979, "Second Thoughts on Keynesian Economics," *American Economic Review*, Vol. 69 (May), pp. 54–59.

Chari, V.V., Lawrence Christiano, and Patrick Kehoe, 1995, "Policy Analysis in Business Cycle Models," in *Frontiers of Business Cycle Research*, ed. by Thomas F. Cooley (Princeton, New Jersey: Princeton University Press).

Cooley, Thomas F., and Gary Hansen, 1995, "Money and the Business Cycle," in *Frontiers of Business Cycle Research*, ed. by Thomas F. Cooley (Princeton, New Jersey: Princeton University Press).

Dixit, Arinash, and Luisa Lambertini, 2000, "Fiscal Discretion Destroys Monetary Commitment," IMF Seminar Series No. 2000-26 (Washington: International Monetary Fund), pp. 1–29.

Economic Planning Unit, Malaysia, *Mid-Term Review of the Seventh Malaysia Plan, 1996–2000* (Kuala Lumpur).

Hemming, Richard, and Murray Petrie, "A Framework for Assessing Fiscal Vulnerability," IMF Working Paper 00/52 (Washington: International Monetary Fund).

Kopits, George, and Steven Symansky, 1998, *Fiscal Policy Rules*, IMF Occasional Paper No. 162 (Washington: International Monetary Fund).

Kydland, Finn E., and Edward C. Prescott, 1997, "Rules Rather Than Discretion: The Inconsistency of Optimal Plans," *Independent Central Banks and Economic Performance* (Cheltenham, England: Elgar Reference Collection), pp. 3–21.

Mackenzie, George A., and Peter Stella, 1996, *Quasi-Fiscal Operations of Public Financial Institutions*, IMF Occasional Paper No. 142 (Washington: International Monetary Fund).

Potter, Barry, and Jack Diamond, eds., 1999, *Guidelines on Public Expenditure Management* (Washington: International Monetary Fund).

Végh, Carlos, and Ernesto Talvi, 2000, "Tax Base Variability and Procyclical Fiscal Policy," NBER Working Paper No. 7499 (Cambridge, Massachusetts: National Bureau of Economic Research).

V Capital Controls in Response to the Asian Crisis

Natalia Tamirisa

Capital controls introduced by Malaysia during the Asian crisis have been a subject of much debate. Contrary to the views that the controls would have serious detrimental effects on the economy, only limited economic costs of the controls have been identified. At the same time, the benefits of the controls cannot be clearly established. Together with the pegging of the exchange rate, the controls had been designed to enhance monetary independence, thereby facilitating economic recovery and providing breathing space for the implementation of structural reforms. Given the return of confidence to the region shortly after the introduction of the controls, however, it appears ex post that Malaysia's strong fundamentals would have made a more accommodating monetary policy and economic recovery possible without resorting to these measures.[1]

It is too early to discern the longer-term effects of the controls on capital flows or on the development of the financial system in Malaysia. If foreign investors expect Malaysia to resort to controls on portfolio outflows in future periods of instability, they may attach a higher risk premium to investing in the country. As for the remaining controls on international transactions in ringgit, these need to be evaluated in the broader context of domestic financial system development and prudential risk management.

Background

In tandem with the pegging of the exchange rate, the authorities introduced capital controls in September 1998, aimed at restricting portfolio outflows and eliminating the offshore ringgit market (Table 5.1). Portfolio investors were restricted from withdrawing funds invested in Malaysia for at least a year, and trading of the ringgit outside of the country was prohibited. Additionally, fund transfers abroad became subject to approval; international borrowing and lending in ringgit, as well as trade settlements in ringgit, were prohibited; and exports and imports of ringgit banknotes were restricted. Capital controls were supported by other regulatory measures, particularly those on trading in Malaysian equities.[2]

As the economic situation stabilized, controls on portfolio outflows were eased and eventually removed. However, controls on international transactions in ringgit remain largely intact (Figure 5.1 and Table 5.1).

The impact of the capital controls appears to have been limited so far. Reflecting in part their easing after less than six months, the controls had only a transitory adverse effect on Malaysia's access to international capital markets and its position in major investment indices. The capital controls appear to have affected portfolio flows to some degree and may have contributed to a decline in foreign direct investment, although isolating the impact of the controls from that of other policies and identifying a proper counterfactual are particularly difficult. It also appears that controls on international transactions in ringgit, which eliminated the offshore ringgit market, helped to reduce speculation against the ringgit at a time of highly volatile exchange markets. The effect of the capital controls on the domestic equity market was mixed, but foreign participation in derivatives markets declined.

The timing of the imposition of these capital controls mitigated their short-term negative impact. They were introduced well into the Asian crisis after a substantial amount of capital had already left the country, and thus their effects on portfolio outflows were limited. By then, the external environment had improved, and market sentiment about the region had reversed for the better. Ex post, the ringgit became undervalued, further reducing incentives for capital outflows. The subsequent easing of controls on portfolio outflows led to the reinclusion of Malaysia in the Morgan Stanley Capital Indices and helped generate new portfolio inflows. Improvement

---

[1]See also Sections II, VI, and VII.

[2]A discussion of capital controls during September 1998–February 1999 can be found in Kochhar and others (1999), Chapter I.

Table 5.1. Key Changes in Capital Account Regulations

Date/Type of Transaction	Measure
January 17, 1994 Bank transactions	A ceiling was placed on the net external liability position of domestic banks, excluding trade-related and direct investment inflows. This was removed on January 20, 1995.
January 24, 1994 Portfolio investment	Residents were prohibited from selling the following Malaysian securities to nonresidents: banker's acceptances; negotiable instruments of deposit; Bank Negara Malaysia bills; treasury bills; government securities (including Islamic securities) with a remaining maturity of up to one year; and Cagamas bonds and notes (whether or not sold or traded on a discount basis) with a remaining maturity of up to one year. This was removed on August 12, 1994.
February 7, 1994 Portfolio investment	Residents were prohibited from selling to nonresidents all forms of private debt securities (including commercial papers but excluding securities convertible into ordinary shares) with a remaining maturity of one year or less.
	The restriction on the sale of Malaysian securities to nonresidents was extended to both the initial issue of the relevant security and the subsequent secondary market trade.
February 23, 1994 Banking system transactions	Forward transactions (on the bid side) and non–trade related swaps by commercial banks with foreign customers were prohibited to curtail the speculative activities of offshore agents seeking long positions in ringgit. This was lifted on August 16, 1994.
August 12, 1994 Portfolio investment	Restrictions on the sale of Malaysian securities were lifted, and residents were permitted to sell to nonresidents any Malaysian securities.
December 1, 1994 Borrowing and lending	Measures were implemented to control borrowing and lending activities in domestic and foreign currency.
	* Nonresident-controlled companies were allowed to obtain credit facilities, including immovable property loans, up to RM 10 million without specific approval, provided that at least 60 percent of their total credit facilities from banking institutions were obtained from Malaysian-owned banking institutions. Short-term trade facilities, guarantees, and forward foreign exchange facilities were excluded from the computation of the RM 10 million limit in December 1994, while the 60:40 rule continued to apply to total short-term trade facilities.
	* Nonresidents with valid work permits were permitted to obtain domestic borrowing to finance up to 60 percent of the purchase price of residential property for their own accommodations.
	* Residents were permitted to borrow in foreign currency up to a total of the equivalent of RM 5 million from nonresidents and from commercial and merchant banks in Malaysia.
June 27, 1995 Portfolio investment	Corporate residents with a domestic credit facility were allowed to remit funds up to the equivalent of RM 10 million for overseas investment purposes each calendar year.
February 1, 1996 Payments for invisible transactions	The threshold for the completion of the statistical forms for each remittance to, or receipt of funds from, nonresidents was raised to RM 100,000 or its equivalent in foreign currency from amounts exceeding RM 50,000.
August 4, 1997 Banking system transactions	Controls were imposed on banks to limit outstanding offer-side swap transactions in ringgit that were non–commercial related (i.e., forward order/spot purchases of ringgit by foreign customers) to $2 million or its equivalent per foreign customer. Hedging requirements of foreigners for trade-related and genuine portfolio and foreign direct investments were excluded.
August 8, 1997 Stock market transactions	A ban on short selling of the listed securities on the Kuala Lumpur stock exchange was introduced to limit speculative pressures on equity prices and exchange rates.
October 15, 1997 Real estate transactions	The quota on sales to foreigners of high-end condominiums was raised to 50 percent from 30 percent, and foreigners were allowed to acquire two units of condominiums (compared with one earlier) to reduce some of the impending supply in the high end of the property market.
September 1, 1998 Offshore ringgit market transactions	A number of selective exchange control measures were introduced, aimed specifically at eliminating the offshore ringgit market and restricting the supply of ringgit to speculators.
	* A requirement was introduced to repatriate all ringgit held offshore, including ringgit deposits in overseas banks, by October 1, 1998; these required Bank Negara Malaysia approval thereafter. An approval requirement was imposed to transfer funds between external accounts and for the use of funds other than permitted purposes (i.e., the purchase of ringgit assets). Licensed offshore banks were prohibited from trading in ringgit assets, which had been allowed up to permitted limits previously.
	* A limit was introduced on exports and imports of ringgit by resident and nonresident travelers, effective September 1, 1998. No prior limits existed.
	* Residents were prohibited from granting ringgit credit facilities to nonresident correspondent banks and stockbroking companies. This had been subject to a limit previously.

Table 5.1 *(continued)*

Date/Type of Transaction	Measure
	* Residents were prohibited from obtaining ringgit credit facilities from nonresidents. This had been subject to limits previously. * All imports and exports were required to be settled in foreign currency. * All purchases and sales of ringgit financial assets could only be effected through authorized depository institutions. Trading in Malaysian shares on Singapore's Central Limit Order Book over-the-counter market was prohibited de facto as a result of strict enforcement of the existing law requiring Malaysian shares to be registered in the Kuala Lumpur stock exchange prior to trade.
September 1, 1998 Portfolio and other forms of investment	A number of additional measures were introduced aimed at preventing heavy capital outflows by residents and nonresidents. * An approval requirement was imposed for nonresidents to convert ringgit held in external accounts into foreign currency, except for purchases of ringgit assets, conversion of profits, dividends, interest, and other permitted purposes. No such restrictions existed previously. There were, however, no restrictions on conversions of ringgit funds in the external accounts of nonresidents with work permits, embassies, high commissions, central banks, international organizations, and missions of foreign countries in Malaysia. * A 12-month waiting period was required for nonresidents to convert ringgit proceeds from the sale of Malaysian securities held in external accounts. This excluded foreign direct investment flows, repatriation of interest, dividends, fees, commissions, and rental income from portfolio investment. No such restrictions existed previously. * A prior approval requirement was imposed, beyond a certain limit, for all residents investing abroad in any form. This was previously applied only to corporate residents with domestic borrowing. * A specific limit was placed on exports of foreign currency by residents up to the amounts brought into Malaysia for nonresidents. Previously there was no restriction on the export of foreign currency notes and traveler's checks on the person or in the baggage of a traveler. Exports by other means required approval, regardless of the amount.
December 12, 1998 Lending in ringgit	Commercial banks and finance companies were allowed to extend loans to nonresidents for the purpose of purchasing residential, commercial, or industrial property, or office space in Malaysia for the period from December 12, 1998 to January 12, 1999, subject to certain conditions.
January 13, 1999 Portfolio investment	Capital flows for the purpose of trading in derivatives on the commodity and monetary exchange of Malaysia and the Kuala Lumpur options and financial futures exchange were permitted for nonresidents, without being subject to the rules governing external accounts, when transactions were conducted through "designated external accounts" that could be created with tier-1 commercial banks in Malaysia.[1]
February 15, 1999 Portfolio investment	The 12-month holding period rule for repatriation of portfolio capital was replaced with two measures: * A graduated system of exit levy was applied on the repatriation on the principal of capital investments—in shares, bonds, and other financial instruments, except property investments—made prior to February 15, 1999. The levy decreased over the duration of the investment, and thus penalized earlier repatriations; the levy was 30 percent if repatriated less than seven months after entry, 20 percent if repatriated in seven to nine months, and 10 percent if repatriated in nine to twelve months. No levy was imposed on the principal if repatriated after twelve months. * A graduated exit levy was applied on the repatriation of profits from investments made after February 15, 1999 in shares, bonds, and other financial instruments, except property investments. The levy decreased over the duration of investment; the levy was 30 percent if repatriated in less than twelve months after the profit was realized and 10 percent if repatriated after twelve months. No exit levy was imposed on capital repatriation. The aim was to preempt the potential exodus of funds in September when the holding period was set to expire, and to encourage fresh inflows to facilitate the recovery.
February 18, 1999 Portfolio investment	The repatriation of funds relating to investments in immovable property was exempted from the exit levy regulations.
March 1, 1999 Export and import of ringgit banknotes	The ceiling on the import and export of ringgit for border trade with Thailand in selected areas was raised.
April 5, 1999 Portfolio investment	Investors in the MESDAQ, where growth and technology shares are listed, were exempted from the exit levy introduced on February 15, 1999.

Table 5.1 *(concluded)*

Date/Type of Transaction	Measure
July 8, 1999 Lending in ringgit	Commercial banks were allowed to grant overdraft facilities not exceeding RM 200 million in aggregate for intraday transactions and not exceeding RM 5 million for overnight transactions to foreign stockbroking companies.
September 21, 1999 Portfolio investment	The two-tier levy system was replaced with a flat 10 percent levy on repatriation of profits on portfolio investment, irrespective of when the profits were repatriated. Bank Negara Malaysia explained there were complaints by foreign fund managers that the graduated system complicated the pricing of their portfolios and that the complex calculation of the amount of the applicable levy raised administrative costs.
September 21, 1999 Swap and forward transactions	To provide foreign investors with more flexibility in managing their portfolios and risks, Bank Negara Malaysia relaxed controls on lending in ringgit to foreign stockbroking companies. Commercial banks were allowed to enter into short-term currency swap arrangements with foreign stockbroking companies to cover payment for purchases of shares on the Kuala Lumpur stock exchange and for outright ringgit forward sale contracts with nonresidents who have a firm commitment to purchase shares on the Kuala Lumpur stock exchange, for a maturity period not exceeding five working days and with no rollover option.
October 4, 1999 Lending in ringgit	Commercial banks and finance companies were allowed to extend loans to nonresidents for the purpose of purchasing residential, commercial, or industrial property, or office space in Malaysia for the period from October 29 to December 7, 1999. This was to support official housing campaigns and was subject to certain conditions.
March 14, 2000 Portfolio investment	Original nonresident holders of securities purchased on the Central Limit Order Book were allowed to repatriate all funds arising from the sale of these securities without payment of the exit levy.
April 24, 2000 Borrowing	In line with the objective of promoting the development of the domestic bond market, resident companies in Malaysia were allowed to issue private debt securities for permitted purposes without prior written approval from Bank Negara Malaysia. Nonresident-controlled companies raising domestic credit facilities by way of private debt securities were exempted from the RM 19 million limit and the 50:50 requirement for issuance of private debt securities on tender basis through the fully automated system for tendering.
June 29, 2000 Portfolio investment	Administrative procedures were issued to facilitate the classification of proceeds from the sale of the Central Limit Order Book securities as being free from levy.
June 30, 2000 Borrowing	Guidelines on private debt securities were issued.
July 27, 2000 Export and import of currency	Residents and nonresidents were no longer required to make a declaration in the traveler's declaration form as long as they carry currency notes and/or traveler's checks within the permissible limits. For nonresidents, the declaration was incorporated into the embarkation card issued by the Immigration Department.
September 30, 2000 Borrowing in ringgit and investment in ringgit assets	Licensed offshore banks in the Labuan international offshore financial center were allowed to invest in ringgit assets and instruments in Malaysia for their own accounts only and not on behalf of their clients. The investments could not be financed by ringgit borrowing.
December 1, 2000 Lending by foreign-owned banks	Foreign-owned banking institutions in Malaysia were allowed to extend up to 50 percent of the total domestic credit facilities to nonresident-controlled companies, in the case of credit facilities extended by resident banking institutions. This is to fulfill Malaysia's commitment under the General Agreement on Trade and Services. Previously, foreign-owned banking institutions could only extend up to a maximum of 40 percent funding.
December 20, 2000 Lending in ringgit	Licensed commercial banks and Bank Islam Malaysia Berhad in Malaysia were allowed to extend intraday overdraft facilities not exceeding RM 200 million in aggregate and overnight facilities not exceeding RM 10 million to foreign stockbroking companies and foreign global custodian banks.
February 1, 2001 Portfolio and other forms of investment	The exit levy on profits repatriated after one year was abolished. Portfolio profits repatriated within one year remained subject to the 10 percent levy.
May 2, 2001	The 10 percent exit levy was removed altogether.

Source: Information provided by the Malaysian authorities.

[1]The classification of tier-1 and tier-2 banks is no longer applicable. As of September 21, 1999, all commercial banks in Malaysia are allowed to open designated external accounts for nonresidents.

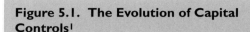

Figure 5.1. The Evolution of Capital Controls[1]

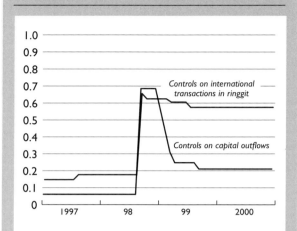

Sources: Information provided by the Malaysian authorities; and IMF staff estimates.

[1]To trace the evolution of capital controls, simple indices are constructed similarly to Tamirisa (1999); and Johnston and others (1999). Indices equal the weighted sum of capital controls in place in a given month normalized by the weighted sum of capital controls introduced since 1991. Weights are assigned as follows: prohibition is given the weight of 1; quantitative limit, approval equirement, or a tax greater than ten percent, the weight of 0.5; and notification requirement or a tax less than ten percent, the weight of 0.2. The indices range from 0 to 1, with higher values indicating more extensive controls.

in investors' sentiment was further enhanced by the authorities' resolve to take advantage of the breathing space provided by capital controls and their pursuit of financial and corporate reforms. Finally, careful design and effective enforcement of the controls helped to focus on their intended objectives, thereby lessening their adverse effects. The controls were selective and did not extend to payments for current international transactions or foreign direct investment. Overall, there appears to be no evidence of a large-scale circumvention, the emergence of a black market, or a nondeliverable forward market.

It is too early, however, to conclude whether capital controls will have any long-term effect on capital flows and financial system development in Malaysia. Foreign investors may view Malaysia's recent resort to the exit levy, and controls on portfolio outflows more generally, as a major reversal of its traditional policy and expect the authorities to repeat this in times of instability. Accordingly, the risk premium on foreign investment in Malaysia may rise. Consideration of the potential usefulness of the remaining controls over the medium term needs to take into account these broader economic costs, as well as their effectiveness. As regards the regulation of international

transactions in ringgit, cross-country experiences suggest that this regulation needs to be considered carefully in the context of a longer-term policy approach to capital account regulation and financial development, particularly the deepening of onshore financial markets.

The remainder of this section discusses the design and enforcement of the 1998 capital controls, followed by a review of their impact on foreign investment, financial markets, and access to international capital markets. A preliminary empirical analysis is presented. Policy considerations relating to the exit levy on portfolio outflows and controls on international transactions in ringgit are assessed in a cross-country context.

Design and Enforcement of Capital Controls

There is no evidence that the controls were circumvented on a large scale, and neither the nondeliverable forward market nor a black market emerged.[3] Incentives for circumvention were generally weak, because ex post undervaluation of the ringgit and improved regional and domestic economic prospects encouraged investors to keep their funds in ringgit.

The design of the controls contributed to limiting their circumvention. They were selective in that they targeted offshore ringgit transactions and portfolio flows, and not current account transactions nor foreign direct investments. Thus, there was no direct reason for circumvention in relation to trade and direct investment transactions. At the same time, the controls covered the targeted types of flows comprehensively whereby all key identifiable channels for the leakage of ringgit offshore and for the access of nonresidents to ringgit funds were closed. Along with the introduction of capital controls, for example, offshore trading of ringgit assets was prohibited (inducing a closure of the Singapore Central Limit Order Book), large denomination ringgit notes were demonetized, and the Companies Act was amended to limit dividend payments.

Additionally, effective enforcement of controls helped reduce circumvention. While their introduction initially led to confusion and uncertainty—in particular, in regard to outstanding contracts in the offshore market—Bank Negara Malaysia subsequently disseminated information on the controls to ensure clarity. Bank Negara Malaysia succeeded in

---

[3]Circumvention could occur, for example, through leading and lagging in the settlement of commercial transactions, dividend payments, intrafirm transfers, or misinvoicing of current account transactions.

Table 5.2. Sovereign Credit Ratings

	Standard and Poor's	Moody's
1998 first quarter	A	A2
1998 second quarter	A–	A2
1998 third quarter	BBB–	Baa3
1998 fourth quarter	BBB–	Baa3
1999 first quarter	BBB–	Baa3
1999 second quarter	BBB–	Baa3
1999 third quarter	BBB–	Baa3
1999 fourth quarter	BBB	Baa3
2000 first quarter	BBB	Baa3
2000 second quarter	BBB	Baa3
2000 third quarter	BBB	Baa3
2000 fourth quarter	BBB	Baa2

Sources: Standard and Poor's; Moody's; and Bloomberg (various dates).

monitoring and enforcing the controls through close collaboration with commercial banks, building on the preexisting relationship with the banks that reflected the fact that many capital account transactions had already been subject to Bank Negara Malaysia approval. Bank Negara Malaysia's reputation as a strict regulator may have also prevented foreign banks from exploring ways to circumvent controls, for fear of losing their local branches.

Capital Controls and Economic Performance

Access to International Capital Markets and Short-Term Financing

The capital controls had an adverse, albeit temporary, effect on Malaysia's access to international capital markets and short-term financing. Following the introduction of the controls in September 1998, international rating agencies downgraded Malaysia's credit and sovereign debt ratings (Table 5.2). Country risk, as reflected in the sovereign bond spread and international credit ratings, increased to a greater extent than the ratings of other emerging markets in the region (except Indonesia), which were negatively affected by Russia's default that had taken place the previous month (Figure 5.2).[4]

Following the easing of controls and a strengthening of the domestic recovery in 1999, Malaysia's

outlook and ratings were upgraded, and the sovereign bond spread narrowed to a level comparable to those of Korea and Thailand. In May 1999, the government issued a ten-year global bond of $1 billion—the first issue in almost a decade—to test investors' sentiment and set a sovereign benchmark in international capital markets. The bond spread was wider than that prevailing at the time for comparable South Korean and Thai sovereign bonds by about

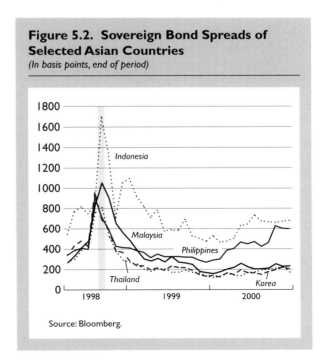

Figure 5.2. Sovereign Bond Spreads of Selected Asian Countries
(In basis points, end of period)

Source: Bloomberg.

___
[4]The increase in the sovereign bond spread caused the government to abandon its original plans to underwrite an international issue for launching Danaharta in November 1998.

140 basis points.[5] The favorable financing outlook in 2000, owing in part to high oil prices, prompted Malaysia to proceed with the issue of its first euro-denominated bond of €650 million and the refinancing of its $1.35 billion five-year sovereign syndicated loan at 52 basis points over Libor, well below its original December 1998 issue price of 290 basis points. In line with developments in its country risk, access to short-term financing was affected by the capital controls, but only temporarily. The decline in short-term borrowing in 1999–2000 was due mainly to repayments of existing loans and lower demand for hedging and trade financing.

Capital Flows

The capital controls appear to have had a limited impact on portfolio flows in 1999–2000. This was largely due to the fact that a substantial amount of capital—about $10.4 billion—had already left Malaysia during 1997–98, before the controls were imposed (Figure 5.3). Thus, outflows that occurred following the easing of controls and the expiration of the one-year holding period were relatively small.

Portfolio inflows increased starting in mid-1999, with the market sentiment turning bullish in response to Bank Negara Malaysia's monetary easing, the upgrading of Malaysia's outlook and credit ratings, and the improvement in the overall regional prospects. The inflows increased further in early 2000, as the rising equity market stirred up investors' interest and political uncertainty related to the November 1999 general elections had dissipated. The prospects for Malaysia's reinstatement in the Morgan Stanley Capital Indices also firmed up, and fund managers who benchmarked against these indices raised the share of their portfolios allocated to Malaysia.[6] Later in 2000, however, portfolio flows reversed, discouraged by a weakening equity market that followed the trends in the United States. All in all, portfolio flows during 1999–2000 seem to have been driven largely by factors other than capital controls. A preliminary empirical analysis shows that the tightening of controls on outflows and on international transactions in ringgit had insignificant effects on portfolio investment so far (Appendix).

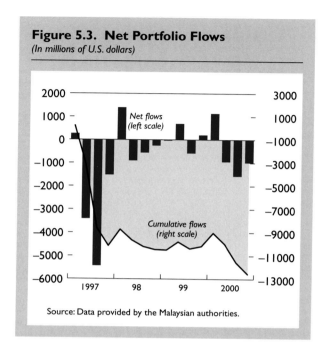

Figure 5.3. Net Portfolio Flows
(In millions of U.S. dollars)

Source: Data provided by the Malaysian authorities.

Despite the explicit exemption of foreign direct investment flows from capital controls and a more liberal policy starting in July 1998,[7] foreign direct investment declined during 1999–2000 to less than half of precrisis levels (Table 5.3). As a share of GDP, foreign direct investment flows fell to the levels observed in other crisis countries, after exceeding them significantly before the crisis. Several factors unrelated to capital controls may have contributed to this decline, including slower growth in Japan and Taiwan Province of China, the worsening of investor sentiment during the Asian crisis, and the decline in overall investment in Malaysia. Capital controls, however, could have exerted an indirect negative effect on foreign direct investment in Malaysia. Foreign investors had reportedly become increasingly concerned about a higher risk of investing in Malaysia, changes in investment regulations, delays and administrative costs associated with additional verification and approval requirements for transfers between external accounts, and more limited hedging opportunities.

Nevertheless, drawing any conclusions regarding the effect of capital controls on foreign direct invest-

---

[5]The bond carried a coupon of 8.75 percent, and was priced to yield 8.86 percent, about 330 basis points above the 30-year benchmark U.S. Treasury yield. It was assigned a BBB senior unsecured rating by Standard and Poor's. The relatively high premium induced the government to reduce the size of the issue by half.

[6]Malaysia was reinstated in the IFC and Dow Jones investment indices in November 1999 and in the Morgan Stanley Capital Indices in May 2000.

---

[7]Measures introduced in mid-1998 to encourage foreign direct investment included allowing total foreign ownership of manufacturing (except in specified sectors), regardless of the degree of export orientation; increasing the foreign ownership share limit in the telecommunications, stockbroking, and insurance industries; and relaxing curbs on foreign investment in landed property.

Table 5.3. Net Foreign Direct Investment in Selected Asian Countries

Country	1996	1997	1998	1999	2000[1]
	(In billions of U.S. dollars)				
Korea	–2.3	–1.6	0.4	5.9	3.7
Malaysia	3.5	3.9	1.9	1.9	1.5
Philippines	1.3	1.1	1.6	0.9	0.5
Thailand	1.7	3.4	6.8	5.8	3.7
	(As a percentage of GDP)				
Korea	–0.5	–0.3	0.1	1.4	0.7
Malaysia	3.5	3.9	2.6	2.4	1.7
Philippines	1.6	1.4	2.4	1.1	0.6
Thailand	0.9	2.3	6.1	4.6	2.9

Source: IMF *World Economic Outlook* (various issues).
[1]Preliminary.

ment from the limited evidence available is difficult. Foreign direct investment is an inherently longer-term phenomenon, and in each country it is determined by a gamut of factors, including the country's policy on foreign equity participation in domestic activities and on investment abroad by residents, and strategy for—and progress with—financial and corporate sector restructuring.

Foreign Exchange Market

The activity in the Kuala Lumpur interbank foreign exchange market declined dramatically during 1999–2000 (Figure 5.4). Controls on international transactions in ringgit eliminated the offshore market, and, together with the exchange rate peg and restrictions against onshore position taking, the activity in the foreign exchange market was limited to trade- and investment-related transactions. Major players in the foreign exchange market were domestic corporations, although many of them relied on natural hedging through matching payables and receivables. The volume of interbank foreign exchange transactions fell by 61 percent in 1999 and by a further 10 percent in 2000, to the level prevailing in 1992. The share of swap transactions fell to about half of total transactions in 1998–2000 from 70 percent in 1997 because the August 1997 restrictions on non–trade related swaps had the impact of lowering trading in the swap market. Transactions in U.S. dollars against the ringgit continued to dominate, but their volume share in total transactions declined to 68 percent in 2000 from 78 percent in 1998.[8]

Equity Market

The capital controls had a mixed effect on the equity market in 1998–2000 (Figure 5.5). The introduction of a one-year holding period for portfolio investment and controls on international transactions in ringgit (particularly on lending to nonresidents) caused an influx of ringgit funds into domestic equities, while at the same time curtailing short selling and capital outflows.[9] As a result, Malaysia's equity market rallied, outperforming other markets in the region during September 1998–January 1999. Equity prices continued to rise in 1999, in line with the domestic and regional recovery. The market was largely driven by local retail buying, in the face of controls on investment abroad by residents. The replacement of the one-year holding period with a graduated levy system in February 1999 had a mixed effect on the equity market. While helping to improve market sentiment, it disrupted activities of fund managers by making portfolio pricing and risk management more complicated. The unification of the levy in the following September, along with the relaxation of controls on offers of credit and swap facilities to foreign stockbrokers, apparently had a positive effect on the market. The major boost came in early 2000 from the prospects for Malaysia to be reinstated in the Morgan Stanley Composite Indices. This effect was short lived, however. Similar to other markets in the re-

---

[8]In contrast, transactions in U.S. dollars against the Singapore dollar increased sharply to 19 percent in 1999 and 22 percent in

2000, from 2 percent of the total volume of transactions in 1998, possibly reflecting the requirement to settle trade transactions in foreign currencies.

[9]At the same time, new requirements on share trading, which were introduced in tandem with capital controls, temporarily hindered trading in American depository receipts for Malaysian companies.

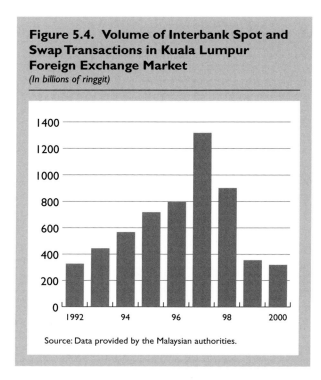

Figure 5.4. Volume of Interbank Spot and Swap Transactions in Kuala Lumpur Foreign Exchange Market
(In billions of ringgit)

Source: Data provided by the Malaysian authorities.

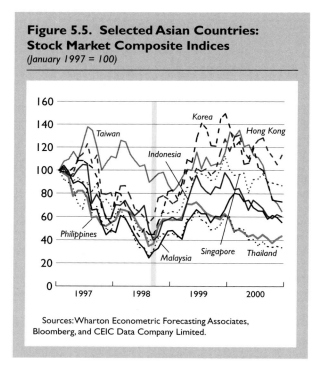

Figure 5.5. Selected Asian Countries: Stock Market Composite Indices
(January 1997 = 100)

Sources: Wharton Econometric Forecasting Associates, Bloomberg, and CEIC Data Company Limited.

gion, the Kuala Lumpur equity market turned in losses by end-2000, in correlation with U.S. financial markets, particularly the NASDAQ, despite favorable domestic developments.

The capital controls appear to have dampened activity in futures and options markets. Foreign participation in these relatively nascent and thin markets declined after the controls were introduced in September 1998 and did not recover even after trading in derivatives was exempted from restrictions on repatriation of capital and profits in January 1999. Economic recovery and the improved market sentiment in other financial markets did not help lift the futures market either. As a result, the average daily trading volume in the Kuala Lumpur Stock Exchange Composite Index Futures on the Kuala Lumpur Options and Financial Futures Exchange (KLOFFE) declined by 44 percent in 1999 and by a further 14 percent in 2000 (Figure 5.6). Trading in three-month Kuala Lumpur Interbank Offered Rated futures contracts on the Commodity and Monetary Exchange of Malaysia (COMMEX) increased to a daily average of 180 contracts in 2000 from 101 contracts in 1998. This increase, however, was mainly due to improved liquidity in the underlying cash market and the decline in interest rates, which encouraged interest rate hedging. The reintroduction of the market-maker scheme in mid-August 1999, which had been discontinued in July 1998, also contributed to the market recovery. Trading was dominated by local financial institutions, and foreign participation declined to 1.2 percent in 1999 from 14 percent in 1998.

Policy Considerations

The Exit Levy

A key control on capital outflows in effect from February 1999 to May 2001 was the levy related to portfolio capital repatriated within a year. There are several arguments for using such a levy to manage capital flows. It is a market-based measure and thus is less distortionary than an administrative control. It targets nondebt, short-term capital flows rather than portfolio flows in general. In principle, the authorities could vary the rate to achieve the appropriate degree of monetary policy autonomy and to alter the level and maturity composition of portfolio flows. As a side benefit, the levy facilitates Bank Negara Malaysia in its monitoring of short-term portfolio flows.

Other things being equal, however, the levy in the form introduced by Malaysia raises the pretax return required by foreign investors. The levy generally cannot be offset by double taxation treaties because it is collected at the time of conversion of ringgit into foreign exchange for repatriation rather than at the time of the transaction; therefore, the full burden of paying the levy, including higher transaction

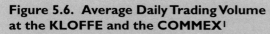

Figure 5.6. Average Daily Trading Volume at the KLOFFE and the COMMEX[1]

(Number of contracts)

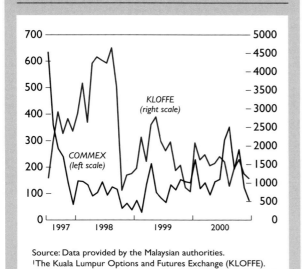

Source: Data provided by the Malaysian authorities.
[1]The Kuala Lumpur Options and Futures Exchange (KLOFFE).
The Commodity and Monetary Exchange of Malaysia (COMMEX).

costs, falls on foreign investors. Since the levy is not indexed to inflation, the required pretax return is increased further. A higher pretax return would imply a higher cost of external financing for domestic firms, thus possibly weakening stock market performance and domestic investment in the longer run.

More generally, even if the levy applies only to short-term portfolio profits, investors may attach a risk premium to investment in the country. The presence of the levy may negatively influence investors' sentiment and discourage portfolio inflows, and such effects are likely to be magnified if the levy is varied frequently. There are also limitations associated with the exit levy, which, without accompanying macroeconomic and prudential policies, is unlikely to be an effective instrument for shifting the maturity composition of capital flows to those of longer term.[10]

The levy may place the country at some disadvantage compared to most other emerging markets. Available data suggest that, until recently, Malaysia was the only middle-income country that taxed repatriation of capital gains from portfolio investment (Table 5.4). When the levy is examined in combination with other taxes, Malaysia's overall taxation on capital gains from portfolio investment still ap-

peared to be more restrictive than that in most other emerging markets, which tend to exempt portfolio investment from both repatriation taxes and capital gains taxes (Table 5.5). This tendency may reflect the emerging markets' efforts to attract foreign investors, in light of the fact that most developed countries do not provide a full tax credit or deduction for capital gains taxes.[11]

Controls on International Transactions in Domestic Currency

During the Asian crisis, the controls on international transactions in ringgit helped abate speculation against the currency. In the context of postcrisis policies, these controls—and particularly their long-term implications—warrant examination from the broader perspective of Malaysia's strategy on financial development and the capital account regime.

Demand for the international use of a country's currency outside of the country depends on international invoicing practices; the level of development of the country's financial institutions, including the breadth and depth of its markets; the regulatory regimes of the financial system and the capital account; and the country's political and economic stability. For an emerging market like Malaysia, there is relatively little demand for the use of its currency as a unit of account in invoicing trade transactions and denominating financial instruments, or as a store of value outside Malaysia, whereby nonresidents hold ringgit as an investment asset. Such demand emanates largely from potential use of the currency within the country, and is limited by international invoicing practices.[12] In addition, the risk preferences of foreign investors influence demand for ringgit-denominated instruments.

Regulations pertaining to nonresidents' ringgit accounts, especially transfers to and from them, have important implications for both international trade and financial transactions in ringgit. In effect,

---

[10]A preliminary empirical analysis shows that prudential measures tended to be more effective than direct capital controls in influencing portfolio investment in Malaysia (see Appendix). For a detailed discussion of effectiveness of controls on short-term capital flows, see Ariyoshi and others (2000).

[11]Notwithstanding the above comparison, definitive conclusions regarding the role of the levy in the cross-country context would require a comprehensive study of investment barriers in the countries concerned, which is beyond the scope of this paper. In this connection, empirical evidence suggests that withholding taxes on dividends are less likely to affect pretax rates of return because the developed countries tend to provide a tax credit or deduction for such taxes (Demirgüç-Kunt and Huizinga, 1995).

[12]Recent empirical studies have identified the following international invoicing practices: (i) trade in differentiated manufactured products between developed countries tends to be invoiced in the exporter's currency; (ii) trade between a developed and a developing country tends to be invoiced in the currency of the developed country; (iii) trade in primary products and transactions in financial instruments tend to be denominated in U.S. dollars; and (iv) exports to the United States tend to be invoiced in U.S. dollars (Tavlas and Ozeki, 1992; and Dominguez, 1999).

Table 5.4. A Summary of Investment Regulations for Entry into and Exit from Selected Markets, end-1998

Country	Entry — Availability of listed stocks to foreign investors	Exit — Repatriation of interest, dividends, profits, and capital
Argentina	Free	Free
Brazil	Free	Free
Chile	Relatively free	Restricted[1]
China	Special classes of shares	Free
Czech Republic	Free	Free
Hong Kong SAR	Free	Free
Hungary	Free	Free
India	Authorized investors only	Free
Indonesia	Relatively free	Free
Israel	Free	Free
Korea	Free	Free
Malaysia	Relatively free	Restricted[2]
Mexico	Free	Free
Philippines	Free	Free
Poland	Free	Free
Singapore	Free	Free
South Africa	Free	Free
Thailand	Relatively free	Free
Turkey	Free	Free

Sources: International Finance Corporation, *Emerging Stock Markets Factbook*; and IMF, *Annual Report on Exchange Arrangements and Exchange Restrictions*.

[1]Unremunerated reserve requirement on debt and certain other flows. Repatriation of capital is free after one year.

[2]The 12-month holding period for repatriation of portfolio capital from September 1998 to February 1999 and an exit levy system from February 1999 to May 2001. For more details, see Table 5.1.

Table 5.5. Taxation of Capital Gains on Portfolio Investment in Selected Emerging Markets, 1999[1]

(In percent)

Country	Top Marginal Rate	Equities[2] Short	Equities[2] Long	Bonds Short	Bonds Long
China	40	Exempt	Exempt	Exempt	Exempt
Czech Republic	32	Ordinary income	Exempt	Ordinary income	Exempt
Hong Kong SAR	15	Exempt	Exempt	Exempt	Exempt
Hungary	40	20	20	20	20
Indonesia	30	0.1[3]	0.1[3]	Ordinary income	Ordinary income
Korea	40	Exempt	Exempt	. . .	. . .
Malaysia	32	Exempt	Exempt	Exempt	Exempt
Mexico	35	Exempt	Exempt	Exempt	Exempt
Philippines	35	0.5[3]	0.5[3]	3–30	3–30
Poland	40	Exempt	Exempt	Ordinary income	Ordinary income
Singapore	28	Exempt	Exempt	Exempt	Exempt
Turkey	55	Exempt	Exempt	Exempt	Exempt

Source: IMF Fiscal Affairs Department, based on data from PricewaterhouseCoopers and Deloitte Touche, Johmatsu.

[1]The predominant tax treatment is indicated.

[2]Listed.

[3]Rate applies to sales value.

Table 5.6. A Summary of Controls on the International Use of Domestic Currency, end-1998[1]

Type of Control	China	Hong Kong SAR	India	Indonesia	Japan	Korea	Malaysia	Philippines	Singapore	Thailand
Controls on the settlement of trade transactions in domestic currency	N	N	N[2]	N	N	Y	Y	Y[3]	N	N
Controls on the import and export of domestic currency notes by residents and nonresidents	Y	N	Y	Y	N	Y	Y	Y	N	Y
Controls on residents' granting credit facilities in domestic currency to nonresidents	Y	N	Y	Y	N	Y	Y	Y	Y	Y
Controls on residents' obtaining credit facilities in domestic currency from nonresidents	Y	N	Y	Y	N	Y	Y	Y	Y	Y
Controls on transfers of domestic currency funds from nonresidents' domestic currency accounts	Y	N	Y	N	N	Y	Y	Y	Y	N
Controls on nonresidents' issuing domestic currency–denominated securities	Y	N	Y	Y	N	Y	Y	Y	Y	Y
Controls on residents' issuing domestic currency–denominated securities abroad	Y	N	Y	Y	N	Y	Y	Y	Y	Y

Source: IMF, *Annual Report on Exchange Arrangements and Exchange Restrictions* (1999).
[1]"Y" indicates yes, "N" indicates no.
[2]Except for member countries of the Asian Clearing Union arrangement, other than Nepal.
[3]Only for export proceeds.

the international use of the ringgit is linked to controls on the settlement of trade transactions in ringgit, on ringgit credit operations, and on the issuance of ringgit-denominated instruments. Regulations concerning Malaysia's offshore financial center in Labuan also come into play, as they determine the extent of "seepage" between international and domestic markets through the offshore center.

Most emerging markets control international transactions in domestic currencies, albeit to a different degree (Table 5.6). The controls are typically effected through approval and reporting requirements, quantitative limits, and sometimes outright prohibitions. Financial transactions tend to be regulated more intensively than trade transactions. In particular, many countries restrict lending to nonresidents in order to constrain their ability to take large positions against the currency. Industrial countries, in contrast, generally have a more liberal approach to international transactions in their currencies, suggesting that a country's level of economic development and the degree of its integration into the world economy are associated with a gradual liberalization of international transactions in domestic currencies.

Experiences in select Asian countries suggest that regulation of international transactions in domestic currencies is generally influenced by considerations related to the effectiveness of monetary control, the scope for nonresidents to take large positions against the domestic currency, and implications for financial development (Boxes 5.1–5.4).

Considerations Regarding the Liberalization of Controls in Malaysia

In Malaysia, a liberalization of controls on international transactions in ringgit requires policy measures to minimize the associated risks. Clearly such a policy should be implemented at a time of relative market stability. Furthermore, in order to limit disintermediation of financial activities off-

---

Box 5.1. Singapore: Reconciling Policy on the Internationalization of the Singapore Dollar and Financial Development Objectives

Since the late 1960s, Singapore has pursued a strategy of developing the city-state into an international financial center, while strictly limiting the internationalization of the Singapore dollar to maintain control over monetary conditions. In the 1990s, controls on the international use of the Singapore dollar were substantially relaxed to promote financial development and facilitate regionalization efforts of the private sector.

Traditionally, Singapore's strategy has been to prevent the internationalization of the Singapore dollar by separating offshore from domestic financial markets and restricting the operations of offshore units. The authorities have been concerned that, given the high degree of openness of the economy, the internationalization of the Singapore dollar will increase the exchange rate volatility and the probability of speculative attacks, and will complicate control over monetary conditions.

Accordingly, banks maintain distinct operations or "units," with separate books and balance sheets, for transactions in the domestic and offshore markets. Domestic banking units may engage in transactions in both foreign and local currencies, and are subject to stringent regulatory requirements and the standard corporate income tax rate of 26 percent. Offshore units, also known as Asian currency units, enjoy a concessionary tax rate of 10 percent and are not subject to reserve and liquidity requirements. Asian currency units focus on operating in the Asian dollar market and are not permitted to transact in Singapore dollars. Offshore banks may accept fixed deposits in Singapore dollars only above S$250,000 and only from nonresidents and other financial institutions. There is a ceiling on lending to residents in Singapore dollars. To limit the short selling of the Singapore dollar and the funding of portfolio and property investments by nonresidents, lending to nonresidents is subject to quantitative limits. Until 1998, loans to residents for use outside the country required approval of the Monetary Authority of Singapore. In sum, the authorities facilitated the participation of Asian currency units in regional banking activities but limited in domestic banking activities.

Over the last decade, the government has eased controls on offshore banks' wholesale operations in Singapore dollars as part of financial reforms aimed at promoting the development of the financial sector. (i) Offshore banks had, since 1973, been permitted to make limited Singapore dollar loans to residents; the relaxation was in response to the argument that restrictions on lending to loyal customers in the domestic market might cost the banks offshore business. With a view to providing more flexibility to offshore banks, the government raised the limit on such lending in the early 1990s (i.e., the maximum amount in domestic loans that offshore banks may have outstanding at any given time) in several steps: to S$100 million in 1993; S$200 million in 1997 (binding the latter commitment in the 1997 Financial Services Agreement of the World Trade Organization); and further to S$300 million in 1998. The limit is expected to be increased further. (ii) Since 1992, banks—including offshore banks—have been allowed to make Singapore dollar loans overseas through their domestic banking units for Singapore-related trade, performance bonds, and for hedging (for imports) purposes. (iii) In August 1998, the government further relaxed some of the restrictions on borrowing in Singapore dollars for use abroad; the Monetary Authority of Singapore indicated that the regulation requiring resident banks to consult them on the overseas use of Singapore dollar credit facilities exceeding S$5 million and on financing of trading activities in Singapore dollar–denominated assets applies only to nonresidents. (iv) More flexible guidelines have been adopted to allow subsidiaries of Singaporean companies and joint ventures between Singaporean and foreign companies to borrow in Singapore dollars for regionalization projects. (v) Finally, foreign entities are now permitted to issue Singapore dollar-denominated bonds for use outside Singapore upon consultation with the Monetary Authority of Singapore and as long as the Singapore dollars are first converted into foreign currencies.

In parallel with liberalizing international transactions in Singapore dollars, the government proceeded with other financial reforms. More competition will gradually be allowed in the domestic retail banking market and, in particular, the 40 percent limit on foreign shareholding in local banks will be lifted. Various measures are being introduced to promote the fund management industry. The focus of prudential policies will largely shift to supervision and, in particular, to the review of banks' risk management systems.

Sources: Cassard (1994); Bercuson (1995); and Cardarelli, Gobat, and Lee (2000).

---

shore, it is important that the onshore financial markets—especially foreign exchange markets—become more liquid and gain more depth and breadth, and that domestic financial institutions become more efficient and resilient. Monetary management also needs to be strengthened because the easing of controls on international transactions in ringgit may speed up the transmission of changes in international interest rates to domestic rates and complicate control over monetary conditions. Additionally, in order to prevent seepage between the domestic economy and the Labuan offshore financial center, the policy of limiting ringgit transactions of Labuan banks needs to be continued, and consolidated bank supervision must be further strengthened.

Box 5.2. Korea: Gradual Liberalization with a Focus on Control of Won Lending to Nonresidents

International transactions in won were liberalized, albeit cautiously and only partially, during 1987–97. In particular, lending to nonresidents was deliberately restricted. The government intends to liberalize the controls further by end-2000 to broaden risk management and investment opportunities for investors and to promote competition in the financial sector. Controls on nonresidents' won funding, however, will remain in place for the next one or two years.

International transactions in won are controlled mainly through approval requirements. While there appears to be no explicit policy against the international use of the won or criteria for allowing these transactions, the authorities are clearly concerned about the potentially destabilizing effects of such liberalization. Starting from 1987, controls on the international use of the won were liberalized as part of the general liberalization of the capital account, but this liberalization lagged behind that of transactions in foreign currency, and approval requirements continued to apply to most transactions even after liberalization. The settlement of trade transactions in won is prohibited, and the export and import of won banknotes are subject to quantitative limits and approval.[1] Rules for nonresidents' won accounts in domestic banks and overseas branches are relatively liberal. The use of won for financial purposes is also controlled through approval requirements. In particular, the issue of won securities abroad by residents and domestically by nonresidents requires official approval. Nonresidents may list shares locally in the form of depository receipts and may issue won-denominated bonds domestically, subject to reporting requirements. The issue of collective investment securities in the domestic market by nonresidents is allowed, provided they establish themselves in Korea and submit a prior report to the Ministry of Finance and

Economy. For residents, the purchase of short-term, won-denominated securities abroad requires Ministry of Finance and Economy approval and prior reporting. To limit potential speculation, credit facilities in won granted to nonresidents by institutional investors of more than W 100 million per borrower require Ministry of Finance and Economy approval.

During the Asian crisis, speculation against the won was limited. In contrast to the currencies of other crisis countries, the won was not overvalued, and the current account deficit was relatively small and manageable. Nonresidents' access to won funds was restricted, and short-selling of the currency became more costly, owing to the initial high interest rate policy. Additionally, the foreign exchange market was relatively thin, as major Korean exporters, the chaebols, tended to hedge in-house by matching receivables and payables. Although there was a viable nondeliverable forward market for won in Singapore and Hong Kong SAR, it was also relatively thin, and position taking there tended to be transparent and costly. An offshore market for the won did not emerge, in part because the authorities allowed the rate to be determined in the market in line with the prevailing flexible exchange rate regime.

In the aftermath of the Asian crisis, the government continued to liberalize the capital account with the aim of broadening investment and risk management opportunities available to investors and enhancing competition in the financial sector. In April 1999, the government streamlined procedures for current account transactions and changed from a positive list system for capital account transactions to a negative one. Offshore transactions in won, nonresidents' won deposits and trust accounts with maturities greater than one year, and offshore and domestic issuance of won securities with maturities greater than one year were decontrolled. Controls on international transactions were relaxed further during the second stage of liberalization by end-2000. Some controls, however, particularly those on won funding of nonresidents, are likely to remain in place for the next one or two years (albeit possibly in a more relaxed form). The authorities are concerned about the reaction of hedge funds to the liberalization and intend to strengthen prudential supervision before continuing the reforms.

Sources: Johnston and others (1999); IMF (1998, 1999); and Park (1998).

[1]Nonresidents are permitted to carry out current account transactions in won, provided remittances are made in foreign currencies. For this purpose, nonresidents may open settlement accounts in won (free won accounts) for current account transactions, reinsurance contracts, and investments in domestic securities.

Policy considerations on this matter must also recognize that the effectiveness of controls on international transactions in ringgit is not guaranteed in the future, particularly in times of instability. The successful experience of the 1998 controls so far is largely due to the appropriate macroeconomic policy mix that prevailed at that time. Even wide-ranging controls, however, are likely to become inadequate in preventing both residents and nonresidents from taking positions against the ringgit if sufficiently

strong incentives were to reemerge. In this case, leakages in capital controls may develop, for example through intercompany accounts, underinvoicing of exports and overinvoicing of imports, leads and lags in transactions related to foreign trade, and small-scale exports of ringgit banknotes. Driven by fundamentals, such position taking against the ringgit may occur illegally onshore, in the newly emerged offshore market, or in the nondeliverable forward market. To the extent that the offshore mar-

---

Box 5.3. Thailand: Relatively Liberal Policy in Normal Times, Temporary Capital Controls to Limit Currency Speculation

Thailand's policy concerning international transactions in baht was relatively liberal before the Asian crisis. In 1997, prior to the floatation of the baht, Thailand imposed temporary capital controls, including those on baht lending to nonresidents, which created a two-tier currency market. These controls were removed for the most part in early 1998.

Controls on international transactions in baht were substantially liberalized in line with the general opening of the capital account during 1989–92. Trade transactions were allowed to be settled in baht. Limits on exports and imports of baht banknotes were relatively generous. Transfers and uses of funds from nonresidents' transferable baht accounts were allowed. Policies concerning baht lending to nonresidents were also relatively liberal.

A widening of internal and external imbalances and a weakening of the banking system induced a series of speculative attacks on the baht beginning in late 1996. The attacks were facilitated by the relatively free capital account, well-developed spot and swap markets, and relatively liberal access of nonresidents to baht credit from domestic banks. Onshore and offshore speculation took place in the form of direct position taking in the forward market and short selling of the currency through explicit baht credits. Investors who were taking positions against the baht included commercial and investment banks, portfolio managers of mutual funds, proprietary trading desks, as well as hedge funds.

To limit speculation against the baht and stabilize foreign exchange markets, Thailand imposed capital controls in May 1997. The measures sought to segment the onshore and offshore currency markets; to limit the supply of baht credit to nonresidents for position taking against the baht; and to raise the cost of carrying positions overnight, while at the same time

allowing foreign exchange conversion for the underlying trade and investment transactions. Financial institutions were required to suspend baht lending to nonresidents through swaps, outright forwards, and sales of baht against other currencies. They were also required to report daily on foreign exchange transactions with nonresidents. Any purchase before the maturity of baht-denominated bills of exchange and other debt instruments required payment in U.S. dollars. Foreign equity investors were prohibited from repatriating funds in baht. Nonresidents were required to use the onshore exchange rate to convert baht proceeds from sales of stocks. Exempt from controls were the underlying transactions related to current account operations, and foreign direct and portfolio investment.

The capital controls created a two-tier market with different exchange rates in the onshore and offshore markets. They squeezed offshore players with short baht positions and forced them to liquidate these positions at a loss, while domestic holders of baht positions apparently maintained their positions. Large differentials emerged between onshore and offshore interest rates, and the swap market dried out. However, the wide differentials created strong incentives for arbitrage, expectations of baht depreciation persisted, and capital outflows continued. Speculation in the offshore market resumed, and eventually in July 1997 the authorities were forced to float the baht.

In January 1998 capital controls were lifted, and the two-tier market was unified. In particular, prohibition of offering baht credit facilities (including—but not limited to—loans, currency and interest rate swaps, options, and forwards) to nonresidents was replaced with a maximum outstanding limit of 50 million baht per counterparty without an underlying trade or investment transaction. Easing of the controls helped improve investors' confidence and contributed to the appreciation of the baht. The enforcement of the new measures was strengthened further in August 1999.

Sources: Ariyoshi and others (2000); and IMF (1998).

---

ket might offer more channels for arbitrage than the onshore market, its presence may accelerate a speculative attack; however, its absence is not a guarantee against position taking. Thus, key to preventing destabilizing position taking is strong fundamentals, especially consistent monetary and exchange rate policies, and effective prudential risk management.

With an easing of controls on international transactions in ringgit, the liquidity of the foreign exchange market is likely to increase as speculators enter the market as risk takers and counterparties of hedgers. The increased liquidity could facilitate portfolio rebalancing and unwinding of leveraged positions; this in turn would help smooth the adjust-

ment of asset prices, facilitate hedging and portfolio management, and generally promote financial market development. Pricing of financial instruments, such that it becomes more reflective of returns and risks involved, will also be made easier, thereby promoting the domestic bond market. In addition, more liberal regulation on credit operations and the invoicing of trade transactions in ringgit may facilitate the regionalization efforts of Malaysian companies in the longer run.

The presence of an offshore market could also improve financial intermediation, enhancing efficiency and investors' opportunities for risk management. Such a market tends to offer a narrower interest rate

Box 5.4. Japan: Toward the Internationalization of the Yen

Japan liberalized cross-border transactions in yen during the second half of the 1980s, in tandem with deregulating domestic financial markets and opening them to foreign participation, strengthening prudential policies, and modernizing monetary policy management. An offshore center was established to promote the international use of the yen.

Until the mid-1970s, Japan's policy was designed to discourage the international use of the yen. The main concern was that substantial yen holdings by nonresidents would jeopardize the Bank of Japan's control over money supply and increase exchange rate volatility.[1] Capital flows and domestic financial activities were tightly regulated.

In response to a slowdown in economic growth and widening budget deficits during the late 1970s–early 1980s, Japan started to deregulate domestic financial markets and the capital account. Interest rates were deregulated, and access of nonresidents to the Gensaki market for repurchase agreements on government bonds and to fiscal bills was liberalized. The positive list system for regulating capital account transactions was replaced with the negative list system in 1980, although many capital controls remained in place.

Cross-border yen transactions were decontrolled during 1984–89. Policy orientation concerning the internationalization of the yen was changed in 1984, after the Yen-Dollar Committee (a working group of Japanese and U.S. officials) and the Ministry of Finance acknowledged the potential role of financial liberalization and the increasing internationalization of the Japanese economy and proposed a program of liberalizing the international use of the yen.[2] Subsequently, the conversion of foreign currencies into yen was de-

controlled. Residents were allowed to lend to and borrow from nonresidents in yen. Controls on the issuance of yen bonds domestically by nonresidents and abroad by residents were relaxed. The market for euro-yen certificates of deposit was created, euro-yen credit operations were liberalized, and the euro-yen market for commercial papers was decontrolled. Foreign banks were allowed to issue euro-yen bonds, and the withholding tax on nonresidents' interest earnings on euro-yen bonds issued by residents was removed. In parallel, domestic financial deregulation continued, monetary policy management was modernized, and prudential policies were strengthened.

In addition to the liberalization of international transactions in yen, the Japanese offshore market was created in 1986 to promote the international use of the yen and to attract euro-yen banking to Japan. Offshore banks were allowed to accept yen deposits from nonresidents, and these deposits were freed from reserve requirements and other controls. By design, the offshore market was separated from onshore banking to prevent "seepage" between them and to ensure the effectiveness of domestic financial regulations.[3] In particular, residents were not allowed to participate in the offshore market, transfers between domestic and offshore accounts were restricted, and loans contracted in the offshore market could not be used to finance domestic activities. In addition, securities transactions were restricted. Since its creation, the offshore market has grown rapidly, becoming a major international center for yen transactions.

The deregulation of foreign exchange transactions and the promotion of the internationalization of the yen continued in the 1990s. Regulations on securities investments and lending, as well as on residents' deposits in foreign banks were liberalized. Withholding taxes on government papers for nonresidents were lifted in 1999 as part of the "big bang" initiative.

Sources: Eken (1984); Tavlas and Ozeki (1992); Dominguez (1999); and Morsink and others (1999).

[1]The loss of monetary control was expected to be less in Japan than in other countries, however, given that the economy was relatively closed.

[2]This was in part aimed at addressing U.S. concerns that the closed nature of Japanese financial markets would artificially depress the value of the yen.

[3]The model of the Japanese offshore market is similar to that of the international banking facilities, which were created in New York in 1981.

spread than the domestic market—where depositors can earn higher returns and borrowers can get access to cheaper financing—because it is not subject to reserve requirements and other regulations; it is a wholesale market and can respond more quickly to investors' needs. Therefore, reemergence of an offshore market could complement the onshore counterpart and provide both domestic and foreign investors access to diversified financial instruments at lower transaction costs and bid-ask spreads. This would allow investors to take advantage of high yields and safe, liquid investments. Owing to its effi-

ciency, the offshore market could be a convenient instrument, especially for large corporations, for holding excess corporate liquidity and obtaining short-term financing for working capital needs.

All in all, the liberalization of controls on international transactions in ringgit needs to be approached cautiously as part of a well-sequenced medium-term strategy of capital account liberalization and financial development. The liberalization of controls on trade-related international transactions in ringgit (e.g., on invoicing of trade transactions) could precede the liberalization of international financial

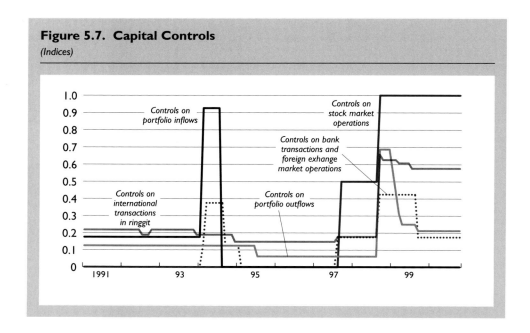

Figure 5.7. Capital Controls
(Indices)

transactions in ringgit. Benefits and risks of the relaxation of controls will need to be carefully assessed, and proper safeguards and supporting policies to control the risks associated with liberalization will need to be put in place. In this regard, a strengthened financial market environment, the maintenance of internally consistent monetary and exchange rate policies, and adequate prudential surveillance are particularly important.

Appendix: A Preliminary Empirical Analysis of Malaysia's Capital Controls

The effect of capital controls on portfolio investment is examined in a simple error-correction model. Portfolio investment is modeled as a function of internal and external factors, including the domestic and foreign interest rates and prices, the real exchange rate, and capital controls.[13] The study covers the period from January 1991 to October 2000, and the evolution of capital controls during this period is shown in Figure 5.7. Table 5.7 describes the data.[14]

[13]The analysis draws on the existing literature on the economics of capital flows. See, e.g., Fernandez-Arias and Montiel (1995); Calvo, Leiderman, and Reinhart (1996); and Cardoso and Goldfajn (1998). For surveys on capital controls, see Eichengreen and others (1998); and Ariyoshi and others (2000).

[14]Data on government expenditures and budget balance are not available on a monthly basis and were not included in the model.

Dickey-Fuller (ADF) tests are used to determine the order of integration for the variables in question (Table 5.8.). Portfolio assets, domestic prices, and the real exchange rate appear as I(1). The domestic interest rate and the foreign interest rate in real terms (*FRR*) are found to be stationary.

Cointegration is tested using Johansen's maximum likelihood procedure with six lags (Table 5.9). The null of no cointegration is rejected in favor of one cointegrating relationship. The recursively estimated eigenvalue is reasonably stable over time. Individual tests on the feedback coefficients imply that the real exchange rate is weakly exogenous, i.e., there is no feedback from the cointegrating relationship to the real exchange rate. Portfolio assets, domestic prices, the real exchange rate, and the trend are all significant in the cointegrating vector.

With weak exogeneity restrictions, the cointegrating vector is given by:

$$CI = pfa - 3.13\ rex - 7.43\ p - 0.01\ trend.$$

The restricted feedback coefficients for *pfa* and *p* are 0.03 and 0.004, respectively. The positive relationship between *pfa* and *rex* and *p* is consistent with economic theory.

Weak exogeneity implies that the cointegrating vector can be analyzed in a two-equation conditional error-correction model, whereby portfolio investment and prices are modeled as changing in response to a disequilibrium in portfolio assets, changes in macroeconomic variables, and capital

Table 5.7. Data

Variable	Description	Source
PFA	Net foreign portfolio assets in Malaysia, billions of U.S. dollars	Estimated based on Bank Negara Malaysia Cash Balance-of-Payments Reporting System and IMF *International Financial Statistics*
REX	Real exchange rate, index	Calculated based on IMF *International Financial Statistics*
P	Consumer price index	IMF *International Financial Statistics*
FP	U.S. consumer price index	IMF *International Financial Statistics*
R	Money market interest rate adjusted for expected depreciation, percent	Calculated based on IMF *International Financial Statistics* and Bloomberg
FR	Eurodollar rate in London, percent	IMF *International Financial Statistics*
CPFIN	Controls on portfolio inflows, index	
CPFOUT	Controls on portfolio outflows, index	
CRM	Controls on international transactions in ringgit, index	Calculated based on the IMF *Annual Report on Exchange Arrangements and Exchange Restrictions* and Malaysia's exchange control regulations[1]
CBNKFX	Controls on bank transactions and foreign exchange market operations, index	
CSM	Controls on stock market operations, index	
ASIA	Dummy variable taking the value of 1 for the period of the Asian crisis, and 0 otherwise	

[1]For more details on the methodology for constructing the capital control indices, see the footnote to Figure 5.1.

Table 5.8. Unit Root Tests[1,2]

H_o	pfa	rex	p	R	FRR
I(0)	−3.16[3]	−1.96	−1.57	−5.23**	−4.15**
I(1)	−3.64*[3]	−8.24**	−8.90**	—	—

[1]ADF statistics are based on the highest significant lag. Constant and trend included.
[2]** (*) indicates significance at the 1 percent (5 percent) level. Lowercase denotes logarithm.
[3]For the period from 1993(3) to 1997(1). Prior to 1993(3) and after 1997(1) *pfa* also appears as I(1).

controls. An autoregressive distributed lag model is reduced to the following parsimonious model through general-to-specific modeling (Table 5.10):

The model is fairly well specified. The goodness-of-fit, autocorrelation, and heteroscedasticity statistics are acceptable. Normality holds. The Chow tests imply constancy.

The results suggest that capital controls (their level and/or changes in them) generally had statistically significant effects on portfolio investment in Malaysia during January 1991–October 2000. The direction and magnitude of these effects, however, varied by the type of capital control. More specifically,

- The regulation of portfolio inflows per se had no significant effects on portfolio investment. The tightening of these controls, however, tended to discourage portfolio investment.

- Controls on portfolio outflows had no significant effects on portfolio investment, neither in terms of their level nor changes in them.

Table 5.9. A Cointegration Analysis[1]

Maximum eigenvalue statistics

	$p = 0$	$p \leq 1$	$p \leq 2$
	30.620**	9.212	6.719

Standardized eigenvectors β

pfa	rex	p	trend
1.000	−3.277	−4.574	−0.015
−2.529	1.000	70.428	−0.194
−0.296	0.715	1.000	0.001

Standardized feedback coefficients α

pfa	0.036	0.007	0.053
rex	0.019	0.007	−0.123
p	0.005	−0.001	−0.003

Tests of weak exogeneity $X^2(1)$

pfa	rex	p
11.420**	2.429	12.445**

Tests of significance $X^2(1)$

pfa	rex	p	trend
5.205*	12.089**	6.646**	8.270**

[1]** (*) indicates significance at the 1 percent (5 percent) level. Constant, trend, and a dummy for 1991 included.

Table 5.10. A Conditional Error Correction Model of Portfolio Investment[1,2]

Variable	Equation for Δpfa_t		Equation for Δp_t	
	Coefficient	t-value	Coefficient	t-value
Δpfa_{t-1}	0.191***	2.610	0.020**	2.108
Δpfa_{t-2}			−0.018	−1.296
Δpfa_{t-4}			−0.067***	−6.245
Δpfa_{t-7}	0.196***	2.618	−0.020**	−2.004
Δpfa_{t-9}	0.275***	3.539		
Δp_{t-9}	−2.342***	−4.012	−0.299***	−4.029
CI_{t-1}	0.058***	2.901	0.004	1.536
CI_{t-2}	0.092	1.372	0.018	1.526
CI_{t-3}	−0.119*	−1.883	−0.011	−0.977
CI_{t-6}			−0.006***	−3.514
Δrex_t			0.060***	5.495
Δrex_{t-2}	0.431**	2.186	0.054	1.450
Δrex_{t-4}			0.045***	4.510
Δrex_{t-9}			0.009	1.067
ΔR_t	0.026**	2.455		
ΔR_{t-1}			−0.010***	−4.795
ΔR_{t-2}	0.034***	2.965	−0.008***	−4.600
ΔFRR_t	−1.714**	−2.456		
ΔFRR_{t-2}	−1.154*	−1.746	0.212**	2.384
ΔFRR_{t-8}	1.706**	2.519	−0.396***	−4.038
$ASIA_{t-6}$			0.003**	2.355
$ASIA_{t-9}$	0.038***	5.012	−0.005***	−3.004
Constant	1.427***	5.046	0.210***	4.126
$CPFIN_t$			−0.004	−1.436
CRM_t	0.052***	3.026	−0.006***	−2.738

Table 5.10 *(concluded)*

Variable	Equation for Δpfa_t		Equation for Δp_t	
	Coefficient	t-value	Coefficient	t-value
$CBNKFX_t$	−0.122***	−4.982	0.013***	2.795
$\Delta CPFIN_t$	−0.087***	−5.599	0.011***	3.481
ΔCSM_t	−0.101***	−3.679	−0.006	−1.547
Single equation tests	Portmanteau = 32.27 AR 1–7 F(7, 58) = 1.94 Normality X^2 (2) = 0.90 ARCH 7 F(7, 51) = 0.48		Portmanteau = 24.10 AR 1–7 F(7, 58) = 1.95 Normality X^2 (2) = 0.51 ARCH 7 F(7, 51) = 0.26	
	Heteroscedasticity test: X^2 (55) = 55.77, F (55, 9) = 0.17		Heteroscedasticity test: X^2 (55) = 50.99, F (55, 9) = 0.15	

Number of observations = 108, 1991(11) to 2000(10).
Full information maximum likelihood estimation. Strong convergence.
Log-likelihood = 1172.235. LR test of over-identifying restrictions: X^2(14) = 12.03.
Vector tests: Portmanteau = 77.07. AR 1–7 F(28, 112) = 1.12. Normality X^2 (4) = 0.94.
Heteroscedasticity test: X^2 (165) = 150.54 and F-form (165, 39) = 0.22.

[1]*** (**,*) indicates significance at the 1 percent (5 percent, 10 percent) level.
[2]The model controls for seasonality and the following time periods: 1991, 1993(11), 1994(1), and 1995(2).

- The regulation of bank operations and foreign exchange transactions tended to reduce portfolio investment. By influencing banks' risk-taking incentives, regulatory measures pertaining to bank operations apparently affected capital account transactions. Controls on swap and forward transactions with nonresidents, in turn, directly constrained hedging and portfolio management opportunities of foreign investors.

- The regulation of international transactions in ringgit had a positive, albeit a relatively small, effect on portfolio investment. This positive effect may reflect the role of these controls in abating speculative pressures on the ringgit. Changes in controls on international transactions in ringgit had no significant effects on portfolio investment.

- The tightening of controls on equity market transactions tended to discourage portfolio investment. The regulation of trading in equities per se had no significant effects on portfolio investment.

The results should be considered only preliminary. Their interpretation is subject to a caveat because the time series used in this study are relatively short to fully reflect effects of the capital controls introduced recently during the Asian crisis.

References

Ariyoshi, Akira, and others, 2000, *Capital Controls: Country Experiences with Their Use and Liberalization*, IMF Occasional Paper No. 190 (Washington: International Monetary Fund).

Bank Negara Malaysia, 2000, *Annual Report 1999* (Kuala Lumpur).

Bercuson, Kenneth, ed., 1995, *Singapore: A Case Study in Rapid Development*, IMF Occasional Paper No. 119 (Washington: International Monetary Fund).

Calvo, Guillermo, Leonardo Leiderman, and Carmen Reinhart, 1996, "Inflows of Capital to Developing Countries in the 1990s," *Journal of Economic Perspectives*, Vol. 10 (Spring), pp. 123–39.

Cardarelli, Roberto, Jeanne Gobat, and Jaewoo Lee, 2000, *Singapore—Selected Issues,* IMF Staff Country Report No. 00/96 (Washington: International Monetary Fund).

Cardoso, Eliana, and Ilan Goldfajn, 1998, "Capital Flows to Brazil: The Endogeneity of Capital Controls," *Staff Papers*, International Monetary Fund, Vol. 45 (March), pp. 161–202.

Cassard, Marcel, 1994, "The Role of Offshore Centers in International Financial Intermediation," IMF Working Paper 94/107 (Washington: International Monetary Fund).

Cheong, Latifah M., 2000, "Evaluation of Capital Controls: Financial and Economic Implications," paper presented at the MIER National Economic Outlook Conference, Kuala Lumpur, Malaysia (January).

Demirgüç-Kunt, Asli, and Harry Huizinga, 1995, "Barriers to Portfolio Investments in Emerging Stock Markets," *Journal of Development Economics*, Vol. 47 (August), pp. 355–74.

Dominguez, Kathryn M., 1999, "The Role of the Yen," in *International Capital Flows*, ed. by Martin Feldstein, a National Bureau of Economic Research conference report, pp. 133–71 (Chicago: University of Chicago Press).

Eichengreen, Barry, and others, 1998, *Capital Account Liberalization: Theoretical and Practical Aspects*, IMF Occasional Paper No. 172 (Washington: International Monetary Fund).

Eken, Sena, 1984, "Integration of Domestic and International Financial Markets: The Japanese Experience," *Staff Papers*, International Monetary Fund, Vol. 31 (September), pp. 499–548.

Errico, Luca, and Alberto Musalem, 1999, "Offshore Banking: An Analysis of Micro- and Macro-Prudential Issues," IMF Working Paper 99/5 (Washington: International Monetary Fund).

Feldstein, Martin, ed., 1999, "International Capital Flows," National Bureau of Economic Research conference report (Chicago: University of Chicago Press).

Fernandez-Arias, Eduardo, and Peter J. Montiel, 1995, "The Surge in Capital Inflows to Developing Countries: Prospects and Policy Response," World Bank Policy Research Working Paper No. 1473 (Washington: World Bank).

Frankel, Jeffrey, 1984, "The Yen/Dollar Agreement: Liberalizing Japanese Capital Markets," *Policy Analyses in International Economics*, Vol. 9 (Washington: Institute for International Economics).

International Finance Corporation, 1999, *Emerging Stock Markets Factbook* (Washington: International Finance Corporation).

International Monetary Fund, 1998, *International Capital Markets: Developments, Prospects, and Key Policy Issues*, World Economic and Financial Surveys (Washington: International Monetary Fund).

———, 1999, *Annual Report on Exchange Arrangements and Exchange Restrictions* (Washington: International Monetary Fund).

Johnston, Barry, and others, 1999, *Exchange Rate Arrangements and Currency Convertibility: Developments and Issues*, World Economic and Financial Surveys (Washington: International Monetary Fund).

Kochhar, Kalpana, and others, *Malaysia—Selected Issues*, IMF Staff Country Report No. 99/86 (Washington: International Monetary Fund).

Morsink, James, and others, 1999, *Japan—Economic and Policy Developments*, IMF Staff Country Report No. 99/181, Revision 1 (Washington: International Monetary Fund).

Park, Yung C., 1998, "Gradual Approach to Capital Account Liberalization: The Korean Experience," a paper prepared for the seminar of the International Monetary Fund on Capital Account Liberalization, Washington, March.

Securities Commission, Malaysia, 2000, *Annual Report 1999* (Kuala Lumpur).

Tamirisa, Natalia, 1999, "Exchange and Capital Controls as Barriers to Trade," *Staff Papers*, International Monetary Fund, Vol. 46 (January), pp. 69–88.

Tavlas, George S., and Yuzuru Ozeki, 1992, *The Internationalization of Currencies: An Appraisal of the Japanese Yen*, IMF Occasional Paper No. 90 (Washington: International Monetary Fund).

VI Financial Sector Issues

Mark H. Krysl and Michael Moore

In response to the Asian crisis, Malaysia undertook a number of policy measures to curtail the deterioration in the financial sector and assist in its recovery. These actions were initiated early and, supported by better domestic and regional economic conditions, have led to substantial improvement in the sector's performance. This section gives a brief background of the financial sector, discusses its performance up to end-2000, and examines key elements of the reforms under way to strengthen its structure and regulatory regime in the context of the Financial Sector Masterplan.[1] Reform aspects that are highlighted include a bank merger program that aims at creating larger and more efficient domestic institutions, and the upgrading of the prudential supervision system.

Background

The financial crisis in Malaysia was comparatively well contained, attributable in part to bank restructuring efforts and the development of domestic capital markets in the 1980s. The country's low foreign debt at the outset also placed it in a relatively good position to confront the crisis. The country's traditional policies to limit short-term borrowing, encourage foreign direct investment inflows, and rely on equity capital prevented the corporate sector from building up excessive unhedged foreign exchange exposures and very high debt/equity ratios that were so damaging in the other crisis countries.

Like the other countries, however, a decade of strong growth prior to the crisis lulled governments and creditors, both foreign and domestic, into complacency. Easy access to bank credit contributed to speculative price bubbles in the real estate and securities sectors, and credit growth in the years leading to the crisis rose substantially, reaching 25 percent annually

in 1996 and 1997. As a result, the level of credit in relation to GDP was high (160 percent), and financial institutions were exposed to those vulnerable sectors. There was, nevertheless, the sentiment that the banking sector in Malaysia was more sound than those in the other crisis countries, because its financial institutions had lower amounts of nonperforming loans and higher capital, and there was a stronger banking culture, with a better supervisory environment, higher standards of accounting and auditing practices, and superior prudential supervision.

Three categories of financial institutions are authorized to take deposits: commercial banks, finance companies, and merchant banks (Table 6.1).[2]

- Commercial banks engage in retail and corporate banking, and are the only institutions authorized to take demand deposits.[3] Through subsidiaries, commercial banks provide other financial services, including merchant banking, stockbroking, insurance, and finance company activities. Foreign banks have operated in Malaysia prior to its independence in 1957. Current regulation limits to 30 percent new equity holdings by foreigners in domestically controlled banks[4] and restricts existing foreign banks from opening new branches.

- Finance companies are able to offer hire purchase lending and other types of installment credit to consumers and small businesses, with funding provided primarily from time and savings deposits. Facing diminishing returns from traditional business lines, finance companies went into riskier real estate and share purchase lending, making them more vulnerable to an economic

---

[1]This section was prepared largely prior to the finalization of the bank merger program and the issue of the Financial Sector Masterplan (March 2001), and includes only a brief outline of those initiatives.

[2]This structure may change further following the completion of the merger process.

[3]Malaysia has two pure Islamic banks, Bank Islam and Bank Muamalat, with total assets of RM 14 billion at end-2000, representing around 2 percent of the banking system assets. They offer Islamic bank products such as interest-free leasing, hire purchase lending, profit sharing, and joint-venture financing. The total market share of Islamic banking assets increased to 6.9 percent in 2000 from 5.5 percent in 1999.

[4]Foreign banks have minority interest in ten domestic commercial banks, three finance companies, and seven merchant banks.

Table 6.1. The Banking System (Depository Financial Institutions)
(In billions of ringgit; as of February 2001)

	Number of Depository Financial Institutions	Percent of Total	Assets	Percent of Total	Loans[1]	Percent of Total	Deposits	Percent of Total
Commercial banks	29	57	516	78	305	76	365	77
Domestic-owned banks	15	29	391	59	233	58	278	59
Foreign-owned banks	14	27	125	19	72	18	87	18
Finance companies	12	24	110	17	77	19	84	18
Merchant banks	10	20	38	6	17	4	27	6
All depository financial institutions	51	100	664	100	398	100	475	100

Source: Bank Negara Malaysia.
[1]Excludes loans sold to Cagamas, the national mortgage corporation.

downturn. Because of the vulnerability, Bank Negara Malaysia began consolidation of the finance company sector early in the crisis, and the process is expected to be accomplished with the completion of the bank merger program.

- Merchant banks are involved primarily in fee-based activities, such as syndication of loans, corporate advisory services, securities underwriting, and portfolio management. They can only accept time deposits greater than RM 200,000. In past years, lending by merchant banks grew to be a key—and at the time profitable—activity, but the diversion proved very costly with a weakening economy. Bank Negara Malaysia has redirected merchant banks back to the traditional fee-based activities by limiting their loan exposures.

Recent Financial Sector Performance

The financial sector, which suffered losses in 1998, has recovered along with the rest of the economy. In 1999–2000, the banking system recorded pretax profits. The recovery can be attributed in part to the restructuring of the banking sector that took place (see below), and in part to a more stable interest rate environment that led to a sharp reduction in loan loss provisions. Nonperforming loans were reduced to 15.3 percent of total loans at end-2000 (Table 6.2). Although asset growth averaged only 4 percent in 1999–2000, there is no evidence of constraints on the supply of credit to the economy, as witnessed by information on loan approvals and disbursements.

- Following a pretax loss totaling RM 8.5 billion during the 12-month period ending March 1999, the banking system began to generate profits in line with the turnaround of the overall economy. The system recorded an aggregate pretax profit of RM 4.7 billion during 1999 and RM 9.7 billion in 2000, with major banking institutions turning profitable.

- The interest margin of the banking system also widened in 1999, reversing the trend of the previous year, and leveled off in 2000. For the commercial banks, the interest margin declined to a low of 3.2 percent in September 1998, owing to locked-in deposit funds in the face of more variable loan rates. The margin improved as interest rates began to fall, reaching 4.5 percent in the final quarter of 1999, but declined slightly to 4.3 percent by end-2000. The margin for finance companies reached a low point of 1.7 percent in June 1998, as deposit rates rose against a high volume of fixed rates for hire purchase loans; since then, the margin grew substantially from the declining interest rates, to about 6.5 percent in 1999 and 7 percent by end-2000.

- Loan growth was flat in 1999 and picked up slowly to 5.4 percent by end-2000. However, taking into account the large amount of loans sold to, or managed by, Danaharta,[5] bad debts written off, and loans converted into private debt securities, the increase in total bank financing has been much larger.

---

[5]See Box 6.1 for a description of Danaharta's role in the restructuring of the banking sector.

Table 6.2. The Trend in Nonperforming Loans[1]

	1997 December	1998 December	1999 December	2000			
				March	June	September	December
(In billions of ringgit)							
Commercial banks	14.2	44.9	40.9	41.7	41.6	42.3	41.6
Finance companies	10.0	24.9	19.1	18.1	18.3	17.9	17.7
Merchant banks	1.1	7.2	5.6	5.1	5.2	5.3	4.3
Total	25.2	77.0	65.5	64.9	65.0	65.5	63.6
Total including loans sold to Danaharta[2]		90.0	100.9	101.3	101.7	102.3	101.3
(In percent of total loans)							
Commercial banks	4.9	15.0	13.8	14.1	13.7	13.7	13.2
Finance companies	9.2	27.0	23.6	22.4	22.5	21.7	21.1
Merchant banks	4.8	32.2	29.6	29.0	29.7	30.5	24.7
Total	6.0	18.6	16.6	16.4	16.2	16.1	15.3
Total including loans sold to Danaharta[2]	0.0	21.8	25.5	25.6	25.3	25.1	24.3

Source: Bank Negara Malaysia.

[1]Loans are classified as nonperforming if payments are overdue for three months or more; prior to January 1, 1998, this period was six months. Total loans include housing loans sold to Cagamas.

[2]Loans were first sold to Danaharta (national asset management agency) beginning in the third quarter of 1998.

Box 6.1. Danaharta: Asset Management and Recovery

Danaharta, a wholly government-owned agency, was established in June 1998 to acquire and manage banks' impaired assets. It has RM 1.5 billion in capital provided by the Finance Ministry, and is authorized to issue up to RM 15 billion (face value) in zero-coupon bonds. RM 11.4 billion in such bonds has been issued.

Danaharta was to purchase nonperforming loans with face values of RM 5 million or more. Financial institutions seeking recapitalization from Danamodal were required to sell their nonperforming loans in excess of 10 percent of total loans to Danaharta as a precondition.

Legislation has vested Danaharta with special power over borrowers, including insulation of the agency (and of subsequent purchasers) from undisclosed claims made after the initial purchase of assets by Danaharta; the ability to appoint special administrators without having to go to court; and the power to abrogate underlying contracts when it forecloses on collateral.

In late 2000, when its window for acquiring nonperforming loans was closed, Danaharta had purchased loans with face values totaling about RM 20.5 billion at market value, as determined by independent auditors, and averaging 45 percent of the face values of the loans. Financial institutions were allowed up to five years to amortize the difference between the book value and the sale price, thereby avoiding immediate recognition of the total loss. In addition, Danaharta has been managing RM 26.2 billion worth of assets owned by the government in connection with government-assisted bank mergers.

Resolution has been reached for 74 percent of the RM 46.7 billion worth of nonperforming loans acquired or managed by Danaharta, involving various workout processes. For viable loans, these include loan restructuring, settlement, and special administration; for nonviable loans, these include sales of collateral, sales of business, foreclosures, liquidation, and special administration via a bid process. The average recovery rate of the loans was 66 percent.

Barring severe external shocks, Malaysian banks are expected to recover at a faster pace than from the previous recession because of less erosion of their asset quality, and because of the authorities' rapid support for, and proactive restructuring of, the banking system (Table 6.3). There are, however, potential vulnerabilities that could slow the recovery. Substantial increases in interest rates could trigger further credit problems for weaker borrowers and create additional nonperforming loans.

Table 6.3. Asset Quality Indicators[1]
(As of January 31, 2001)

	Nonperforming Loans[2]		Nonperforming Loans to Loans		Total Bad-Debt Provision to Nonperforming Loans[3]	
	3-month	6-month	3-month	6-month	3-month	6-month
	(In billions of ringgit)		(In percent)			
Commercial banks	40.9	32.5	13.0	10.3	57.3	66.4
Finance companies	17.9	13.5	21.2	16.0	51.9	62.1
Merchant banks	3.9	3.0	22.4	17.2	41.0	52.6
Banking system	62.7	49.0	15.1	11.8	54.8	64.3

Source: Bank Negara Malaysia.

[1]Including loans sold to Cagamas with full recourse.

[2]Nonperforming loans are shown gross of interest in suspense. Malaysian accounting calls for the continued accrual of interest on nonperforming loans with an offsetting provision to the interest-in-suspense account. The interest-in-suspense balance is a provision equal to the amount of interest accrued but not collected from nonperforming loans. Indicators are shown here for classifications of loans as nonperforming after payments are overdue for three months and six months.

[3]Total bad-debt provision equals the aggregate of provisions for general, specific, and interest in suspense.

Financial Sector Restructuring: Comparative Perspective

In response to the Asian crisis, the affected countries—despite different initial conditions and the approaches they used—adopted similar policies aimed at improving the structure of the financial sector and lessening its vulnerability (Table 6.4). To prevent a collapse of the system, all countries provided a blanket deposit guarantee and liquidity support to financial institutions. Subsequently, each country adopted some form of asset management strategy to address nonperforming loan problems, assigned high priority to upgrading supervisory and regulatory standards to international best practices, and sought to recapitalize financial institutions based on those norms. In the process, bank closures or merger programs were undertaken to establish stronger financial systems. Also, standards of corporate governance were upgraded.

Malaysia has achieved considerable progress in implementing these reforms in comparison to the other crisis countries. The approach adopted by Malaysia (and also by Korea) in resolving bad loan problems and restructuring banks involved a high degree of government involvement, which had the advantages of speed and coherence, notwithstanding the possibility that it could also raise expectations of future government bailouts. Malaysia's efforts also benefited from the country's relatively strong initial position, including its well-developed legal and institutional frameworks. Reflecting these efforts, the financial sector indicators, as measured by nonperforming loans and capital adequacy ratios, have improved in all countries, but those in Malaysia compare favorably (Table 6.5).

Financial and Corporate Debt Restructuring

Malaysia's initiatives to restructure financial and corporate debt in a coordinated way entailed the establishment of Danaharta to acquire nonperforming loans and help banks clear their balance sheets, Danamodal to recapitalize banks (Box 6.2), and the Corporate Debt Restructuring Committee to facilitate debt workout by large borrowers (Box 6.3).[6] This multipronged approach has proved to be a credible plan in the restructuring of Malaysia's financial sector.

Danaharta's broad legal mandate helped ensure that nonperforming loans would be dealt with promptly, while its setup under the Companies Act

---

[6]Korea also adopted a centralized approach to asset resolution and bank recapitalization from the outset, with active government involvement. In contrast, Thailand aggressively liquidated the impaired assets of closed finance companies through a central agency, but it did not permit public sector purchases of impaired assets from private commercial banks. Instead, each bank was encouraged to establish its own asset management company. Following a change in the government in 2001, however, Thailand announced that it would establish a centralized asset management company.

Table 6.4. Financial Sector Restructuring in Malaysia, Korea, and Thailand

	Malaysia	Korea	Thailand
Initial government response			
Establishment of an overarching restructuring authority	Yes[1]	Yes	Yes
Establishment of a separate bank restructuring authority	Yes (Danamodal)	No	No
Liquidity support (in billions of U.S. dollars)	9.2	23.3	24.1
(In percent of GDP)	13	5	20
Introduction of a blanket guarantee	Yes	Yes	Yes
Deposit insurance[2]	No	No	No
Financial distress resolutions			
Bank closures	0	0	1 of 15
Elimination or dilution of current shareholder stakes of insolvent banks	Yes	Yes	Yes
Closure of other financial institutions	0	Over 200	57 of 91
Mergers or interventions	Yes, 54 to be merged into 10 groups by 12/00	Yes, 8 of 26 absorbed by other banks	Yes, 5 banks and 13 finance companies,[3] also 3 banks privatized
Bank recapitalization strategies			
Public funds for recapitalization	Danamodal injected $7.1 billion into 10 institutions	Government injected $36 billion into 9 commercial banks; 5 out of 6 major banks now 90 percent controlled by state	Government injected about $11 billion into public banks
Majority foreign ownership of banks	Control of domestic banks not allowed; foreign bank share is, however, significant[4]	1 announced; 1 pending[5]	4 completed; 2 pending[6]
Instruments used to recapitalize and purchase nonperforming loans	Bonds or cash	Bonds or cash	Debt-to-equity conversions
Asset resolution strategies			
Establishment of a centralized asset management corporation	Yes (Danaharta)[7]	Yes (KAMCO)[8]	No, but an asset management company is planned[9]
Operational autonomy of restructuring agencies	Yes	Yes	Not applicable
Centralized asset management companies purchased assets at subsidized prices	Purchased assets are valued by independent outside auditors	Assets initially purchased above market-clearing prices with recourse. Since 1998, purchase endeavors at market prices	Not applicable
Nature of agency; restructuring or disposition	Restructuring	Not clearly defined; mostly disposal of assets	Not applicable
Eligibility of loans	All financial institutions, including Labuan subsidiaries of Malaysian banks and development financial institutions	All financial institutions	Finance companies thus far, but also banks subject to intervention

Sources: Information provided by country authorities; Claessens and others, 1999, "Financial Restructuring in East Asia: Halfway There?" Financial Sector Discussion Paper No. 3 (Washington: World Bank); Lindgren and others, 2000, "Financial Sector Crisis and Restructuring: Lessons from Asia," IMF Occasional Paper No. 188 (Washington: International Monetary Fund).

[1]Steering committee chaired by the central bank.

[2]Under consideration in Malaysia and Korea.

[3]Between government-owned institutions in which the government has intervened.

[4]Foreign banks are allowed to purchase up to 30 percent equity of domestic banks.

[5]From 15 percent to 100 percent.

[6]Approval required from Board of Investment.

[7]Assets transferred; loans larger than RM 5 million and mostly loans secured by property or shares.

[8]The powers and resources of a preexisting asset management company were substantially increased; worst assets were to be transferred.

[9]Nonperforming loan workout is decentralized. Three banks have established private asset management companies and more are being considered. Hybrid approach to reprivatization of banks subject to intervention is evolving. Thailand has announced that it will establish a centralized asset management company.

Table 6.5. Selected Financial Indicators of the Asian Crisis Countries

	Malaysia[1]	Indonesia[2]	Korea[3]	Philippines[4]	Thailand[5]
Nonperforming loans of the banking system (as a percent of total loans)					
December 1997	6.0	8.4	6.1	4.7	22.6
December 1998	18.6	48.6	7.4	10.4	45.0
December 1999	16.6	32.9	8.3	12.3	38.9
December 2000	15.3	25.6	5.6	15.1	17.9
Risk-weighted capital ratio(s) of the banking system					
December 1997	10.5	8.0	7.0	15.9	9.9
December 1998	11.8	−11.6	8.2	17.5	10.9
December 1999	12.5	−2.4	10.8	17.0	15.3
December 2000	12.4	12.7	10.3	15.8	12.4
Total outstanding bad-debt provision(s) of the banking system (as a percent of nonperforming loans)					
December 1997	66.2	39.6	23.7	42.1	...
December 1998	42.4	40.4	59.6	36.4	21.8
December 1999	50.2	29.0	75.4	45.1	32.2
December 2000	53.8	...	84.7	43.6	...

Sources: Data provided by the country authorities; and IMF staff estimates.

[1]Nonperforming loans include those with interest in suspense and specific provisioning, and are defined as loans for which payments are overdue for three months or more.

[2]Including Rp 254 trillion worth of nonperforming loans transferred to the Indonesian Bank Restructuring Agency; nonperforming loans of the banking system totaled 65.1 percent at end-March 2000. The capital ratio data are equity (as declared by banks) as a percent of total (unweighted) assets (data for 2000 relate to October).

[3]For nonperforming loans, commercial banks' data are used (based on delinquency); December 1997 data include past-due loans over six months and bankruptcy loans; December 1998 data include past-due loans over three months and bankruptcy loans; December 1999 data include past-due loans over three months and nonaccrual loans reflecting forward-looking criteria. Risk-weighted capital ratio for December 1999 also reflects the application of new forward-looking criteria. Total outstanding bad-debt provisions of the banking system data show total provisions on balance sheet as a percent of nonperforming loans.

[4]Nonperforming loan data are commercial banks' data. Capital ratios of the banking system are not risk weighted, based on Basel guidelines. Regulations are being drafted in order to bring the practice into line with the guidelines, in accordance with recently passed legislation. The 2000 nonperforming loan data are for September 2000.

[5]Nonperforming loans include those for Thai private and state-owned banks. Capital ratios for Thailand are based on phased-in provisioning rules, as allowed by Bank of Thailand, scheduled to be fully met at end-2000. Total outstanding bad-debt provision data for December 1998 and December 1999 are balance sheet loan-loss provisions, and do not include surplus capital in excess of the regulatory minimum.

meant that it would be managed as a private entity, subject to normal auditing. The key issue in asset purchases by Danaharta was realistic valuations to ensure that it did not become a tool for indirect bailouts of existing shareholders, which would undermine the incentives for private sector recapitalization and proper governance of the agency and the banks. There are indications that loan valuations by Danaharta were reasonable, although some latitude was given to banks in that the losses on the sales of their assets to the agency could be amortized over five years rather than recognized immediately.

Overall, the plan for Danaharta was well conceived, with nonperforming loans being taken over to ease bank operations. Concentration on larger nonperforming loans (involving only 2,000 to 3,000 accounts) meant that the process was manageable. Furthermore, the emphasis on resolution of nonperforming loans—and not simply their disposal—assisted in the restructuring of the corporate sector. There are, nevertheless, risks of the agency becoming a warehouse for nonperforming loans unless assets are upgraded and sold before long.

The mandate of Danamodal inspired confidence that all domestic financial institutions would be recapitalized to the required standards, maintaining the safety and soundness of the banking sector. The requirement that institutions seeking Danamodal's capital would have to sell nonperforming loans in excess of the specified proportion to Danaharta gave banks the incentive to deal with their bad assets in a timely and coherent manner. Danamodal achieved

Box 6.2. Danamodal: Bank Recapitalization

Danamodal was established in July 1998 with the main objective of recapitalizing the banking system. Capital injections from Danamodal were destined to enable institutions to restore their capital adequacy ratios to 9 percent. To fund its needs, Danamodal raised RM 10.7 billion, comprising RM 3 billion in paid-up capital from Bank Negara Malaysia, and RM 7.7 billion raised through the issuance of zero-coupon bonds to financial institutions.

Selection of candidates for recapitalization was initially guided by Bank Negara Malaysia's watchlist, based on stress tests of banking institutions. Danamodal's participation was also determined by the nonfeasibility of market solutions, the systemic impact of the failure, and the future viability and competitive positioning of concerned institutions. The "first loss" principle, by which original shareholders' equity is written down, is applied strictly to all transactions.

Institutions requesting capital injections must submit recapitalization plans and are subject to monthly reporting of performance against a list of targets. Danamodal exercises control over management by appointing at least two members to the boards of directors, of which one is to be an executive director or chairman of the board.

Ten institutions received a total capital injection of RM 7.1 billion, initially in the form of tier-two subordinated debt that, per definitive agreement, is to be converted into equity; irredeemable, noncumulative convertible preference shares; and/or subordinated loans, depending on the cash flow characteristics of the instrument and circumstances of the banking institution. Eight of the ten institutions receiving assistance have fully repaid their loans. Danamodal's excess funding has gone unneeded because undercapitalized institutions were able to restore capital on their own.

Box 6.3. Corporate Debt Restructuring Committee

The Corporate Debt Restructuring Committee was established in July 1998 to help mediate voluntary out-of-court restructuring of large debt involving a number of major creditors, following the London Rules model. Debt restructuring under the Committee is reserved for viable businesses and not those in receivership or liquidation. Aggregate bank loans must be RM 50 million or more, with at least three lending institutions participating, and the creditor committees representing the interests of at least 75 percent of total debt of all creditors.

The Corporate Debt Restructuring Committee has no legal status, but debt restructuring under its auspices is facilitated by a joint public-private sector steering committee appointed by Bank Negara Malaysia, which is assisted by a secretariat set up in Bank Negara Malaysia. Over 70 companies applied to the Committee for workout arrangements, with debts totaling RM 39.4 billion. The majority were property, construction, and diversified holding companies. At end-2000, 21 of these applications with debts of RM 7.8 billion had been withdrawn or rejected; 42 applications with debts of RM 27.3 billion have been completed or resolved with assistance from Danaharta; and 12 applications with debts of RM 12.1 billion are outstanding.

Debt restructuring in Malaysia has taken a number of forms. The approach taken by the Corporate Debt Restructuring Committee was intended to minimize losses to creditors and company shareholders through coordinated debt workouts that avoid placing viable companies into liquidation or receiverships, and to have banking institutions play a greater role in the financial rehabilitation of the corporate sector.

Prudential Accounting Standards

Prudential accounting standards have been brought closer to compliance with international best practices for all crisis countries. The valuation of nonperforming loans was hampered by the lack of clear market values and continuously changing economic conditions. To better support the valuation process, all countries tightened their rules for loan classification, loss provisioning, income recognition, and collateral valuation, and they have substantially strengthened supervisory scrutiny of compliance by bankers and auditors with these rules. In the case of Malaysia, these changes took place in early 1998 (Table 6.6).

Toward a More Resilient Banking Sector

As the next step in reforming the financial sector, the Financial Sector Masterplan was issued in March 2001. The plan has a long-term vision "to develop a more resilient, competitive, and dynamic banking

its goal of restoring the financial industry's capital level to above precrisis levels. Also, no systemic banking failure was encountered, and the payment system functioned smoothly throughout the crisis.

Table 6.6. Changes in Prudential Standards in Malaysia, Korea, and Thailand

	Malaysia	Korea	Thailand
Date when changes took effect	1/1/98	6/30/98	3/31/98
Loan classification: days elapsed before considered past due	180 days, with parallel classification of 90 days for supervision purpose	Reduced to 90 days from 180 days	Reduced to 90 days from 360 days
Present criteria for classifying			
substandard	6 months	3 months	3 months
doubtful	9 months	3 months	6 months
loss	12 months	12 months	12 months
Loan-loss provisioning (in percent)			
substandard	to 20 from 0	20	to 20 from 15–20
doubtful	50	to 50 from 75	to 50 from 100
loss	100	100	100
Interest accrual	No change, that is, accrual for 6 months maximum	Reduced to 3 months maximum from 6 months maximum	Reduced to 3 months maximum from 6 months maximum

Source: Data provided by the country authorities.

system with best practices, that supports and contributes positively to the growth of the economy throughout the economic cycle, and has a core of strong and forward-looking domestic financial institutions that are more technologically driven and ready to face the challenges of liberalization and globalization."[7] The plan will be a blueprint for the financial sector for the next ten years and will focus on a series of best practices for the industry, as well as initiating a process of corporate governance based on effective risk management. In addition, the capital market is to have a more important role in the allocation of resources.

The main thrust of the plan is to develop strong domestic banking institutions that form the core of an efficient, effective, and stable financial sector. They will be expected to operate in an environment of emerging new technological advances and more differentiated and demanding consumers, and to provide a more diversified range of financial services. The banking sector will not only serve a more internationally integrated and dynamic economy, it should also have a leading role within this economy.

The broad strategies for the banking sector within the plan are to manage the process of liberalization, including the positioning of domestic financial institutions vis-à-vis foreign institutions; to strengthen the financial sector in the wake of glob-

alization and technological advances; and to identify the optimal supervisory philosophy to be adopted within the existing structure, where Bank Negara Malaysia remains the sole regulatory authority of the banking system. Two key components of the plan are the bank merger program and significant changes to regulation and supervision, in line with best practices.

The Bank Merger Program

For all crisis countries, the strategies for systemic restructuring have sought to restore the financial systems to soundness as soon as possible. The process involves the introduction of the legal, institutional, and policy frameworks necessary for dealing with nonviable financial institutions, strengthening viable ones, and resolving value-impaired assets in the system.

Malaysia has undertaken to deal with its banking problems through a comprehensive bank merger program, designed to take advantage of economies-of-scale, to tap potential synergies, and to determine an exit strategy for the weakest banks. In the process, domestic banks were given broad flexibility to form their own merger groups, which total ten, each comprising a commercial bank, a finance company, and a merchant bank (with the exception of one group). Each group is required to have a minimum capitalization of RM 2 billion by end-2001, implying the asset size of most banking groups to be in excess of RM 25 billion (Table 6.7).

---

[7]Bank Negara Malaysia, 2001, "The Financial Sector Masterplan" (Kuala Lumpur), March.

Table 6.7. Proposed Banking Groups
(Mergers and acquisitions completed or close to completion as at December 31, 2000)

Anchor Banks	Commercial Banks	Finance Companies	Merchant Banks	Assets of Anchor Banks (in RM billion)[1]	Post-Merger Assets (in RM billion)[1]	Percentage of System Assets
Maybank	Pacific Bank PhileoAllied Bank	Mayban Finance Kewangan Bersatu Sime Finance	Aseambankers Malaysia	106	145	28.2
Bumiputra-Commerce Bank		Bumiputra-Commerce Finance	Commerce International Merchant Bank	58	68	13.2
RHB Bank		Interfinance RHB Delta Finance	RHB Sakura Merchant Bankers	49	53	10.3
Public Bank	Hock Hua Bank	Public Finance Advance Finance	Public Merchant Bankers	33	52	10.1
Arab-Malaysian Bank		Arab-Malaysian Finance	Arab-Malaysian Merchant Bank	11	41	8.0
Hong Leong Bank	Wah Tat Bank	Hong Leong Finance Credit Corporation		23	40	7.8
Alliance (Multi-Purpose) Bank	International Bank Malaysia Sabah Bank	Sabah Finance Bolton Finance	Bumiputra Merchant Bankers Alliance Merchant Bank	15	20	3.9
Affin Bank	BSN Commercial Bank	Asia Commercial Finance BSN Finance	Perwira Affin Merchant Bankers BSN Merchant Bank	23	32	6.2
Southern Bank	Ban Hin Lee Bank	Perdana Finance Cempaka Finance United Merchant Finance	Perdana Merchant Bankers	17	25	4.9
EON Bank	Oriental Bank	EON Finance City Finance Perkasa Finance	Malaysia International Merchant Bankers	15	25	4.9
Others not yet merged	Bank Utama	MBf Finance	Utama Merchant Bank	...	13	2.5

Source: Bank Negara Malaysia.
[1] As at February 28, 2001.

The merger and acquisition phase was largely completed by end-2000, but much remains to be done. Cultural adaptation alone could present barriers to a quick and smooth progression of the process. Selection of management teams will be critical where there is no clear choice of chief executive officer or chief operating officer already in place. Bank Negara Malaysia requires that each banking group employ an independent consulting firm to advise and recommend individuals best qualified to manage the company. Bank Negara Malaysia will also closely monitor the performance of the banks' management teams to ensure that any identified weaknesses are addressed in a timely manner. In this regard, strategic plans and integration issues for each banking group are important.

- *Integration plans.* An important segment of integration is "cultural changes," namely, blending the cultures of two or more entities.

- *Strategic plans.* Such plans are needed to prevent several banking groups from concentrating on the same market sectors.

- *Staffing.* This issue deals not only with over-staffing and retraining and/or early retirement of excess staff, but also with keeping and developing key individuals to manage the "new" banking system for the future.

- *Information technology.* The integration of two or more data systems must be compatible and efficient, resulting in little or no turmoil to internal operations and consumer interests.

The bank merger program in Malaysia, ambitious in nature and timing, presents short- and longer-term challenges. The reduction to 10 groups from over 60 banks (precrisis) is significant, but the distribution in terms of asset size will initially be disproportionate. Three of the new banking groups will each comprise 5 percent or less of total banking assets, less than one-fifth the size of the Maybank group. Some of the smaller banking groups may not achieve the desired efficiencies or economies-of-scale, creating competitive mismatches with their larger counterparts.

The possibility for additional mergers in the future could also be triggered by a liberalization of the financial services industry to allow for more foreign competition and competitive factors, that is, for larger companies to dominate specific segments.[8] This possibility needs to be watched closely because the improved ability to compete is a key goal of the bank merger program and the Financial Sector Masterplan. There is also a concern regarding the management of some of the new banking groups, namely, depth of experience and strengths to manage a more complex and larger entity in a highly competitive environment.

Prudential Supervision and Regulation

Malaysia moved rapidly to strengthen the framework of prudential supervision and regulation (Table 6.8). In particular, the requirement that banks establish internal systems to manage risks, including for cross-border transactions, and Bank Negara Malaysia's move toward risk-based and consolidated supervision are major steps to enhance the soundness of the financial system, especially as the merger program is completed and financial innovations are embraced by banks in Malaysia.

- Risk-based supervision—with supervisory attention for weak institutions—will allow Bank Negara Malaysia to focus its resources on the most critical areas in the individual institutions, as well as on the stratification of risk areas across the financial sector. The impending requirement for

banking institutions to have formalized risk-management systems is most important in that it will create an environment of self-supervision for the industry and enhance risk-based supervision. Stronger risk-management capabilities of banking institutions, in turn, will render risk-based supervision more effective. Implementation of formalized risk management at the holding company level will further improve the systems.

- Improvements of the systems' risk management have so far included requirements related to derivative products management and liquidity framework (implemented), and credit risk management (scheduled to be formalized by mid-2000). Internal risk-management systems would entail guidelines for other types of risks, in connection with interest rates, foreign exchange, transactions, strategy, reputation, prices, and other types of risks deemed significant to the oversight of each bank's risk propensity.

- A bank-by-bank early warning system currently being developed by Bank Negara Malaysia will provide leading indicators for supervisory attention and allow for preventive measures against the catastrophic deterioration of individual institutions and the overall financial sector. The system, based on an individual bank failure model, will serve to enhance confidence in the financial sector.

- Consolidated supervision is expected to play an important role as the bank merger program is completed, with the new banking groups becoming larger and more complex, and engaging in more varied activities. It will help contain overleveraging by financial institutions. For consolidated supervision to be operative, Bank Negara Malaysia will need to have supervisory mandates over financial institutions' holding companies and other subsidiaries and affiliates. An amendment to the Bank and Financial Institutions Act would be warranted to include the scope of permissible activities for these entities, their minimum capital requirements, approval of dividends by the authorities, and approval for the publishing of reports and appointment of directors.

- Increased transparency of macro- and microeconomic data and policies will help ensure more effective supervision. Similar to the other crisis countries, Malaysia is gradually implementing policies to foster improved corporate governance and lower corporate leverage. Ongoing attention is also needed to improve protection for outside investors through stronger enforcement

---

[8]The share of banking system assets controlled by foreign banks increased to 19 percent in 2000 from around 15 percent in 1997. The government's share of the banking system has also increased over this period, through increased government equity holding and the recapitalization process.

Table 6.8. Steps to Improve Prudential Supervision and Regulation in Malaysia, Korea, and Thailand

	Malaysia	Korea	Thailand
Development of an overall plan and/or strategy for the supervision and regulation of the industry	Yes Masterplan[1]	Under consideration[2]	Yes[3]
Steps to develop and implement consolidated supervision	In process[4]	Under consideration[5]	Under consideration[6]
Steps to develop and implement risk-based supervision	Yes[7]	Yes[8]	Yes[9]
Requiring banks and holding companies to develop and implement formal risk-management processes	Yes[10]	Unknown[11]	Early stages of development[12]

Source: Information provided by country authorities.

[1]The Financial Sector Masterplan was released in March 2001; it sets broad goals for the supervision and regulation of the industry.

[2]Through the refinancing of a World Bank loan, Korea is in the process of securing an outside consulting firm to assist in developing a plan to bring its supervision and regulation function in step with current worldwide standards.

[3]A complete reengineering of the supervision group is under way. As part of the reengineering process, actions to ensure compliance with international standards and the Core Principles are under way.

[4]Bank Negara Malaysia is moving toward consolidated supervision. A change to existing banking law will be required to give Bank Negara Malaysia the authority.

[5]Consolidated supervision is to be considered as part of an overall plan.

[6]Through the proposed Financial Institutions Law and new supervisory policies and procedures, consolidated supervision is being considered.

[7]Risk-based supervision was in the implementation stage when the crisis emerged, and is now being reintroduced into the examination process.

[8]Risk-based supervision will be part of an overall plan for the supervision and regulation of the financial services industry.

[9]Risk-based supervision approach is embodied in all new policies, procedures, regulations, and other supervisory guidelines that are developed. A risk-based supervisory approach for on-site examination is in the testing stage.

[10]Bank Negara Malaysia is moving the industry toward formalized risk-management processes. This is evidenced by the implementation of mandated risk-management practices for derivatives, liquidity, and credit.

[11]The consultant's plan does not specifically address this issue.

[12]New regulations to accompany the proposed Financial Institutions Law will require appropriate risk-management processes.

of disclosure requirements and shareholder and creditor rights.

Other Initiatives

In April 2000, the authorities announced a consolidation plan for the stockbroking industry to reduce the number of companies to 15 from the present 63, in conjunction with a reduction in transaction commissions, although the stipulation of the final number of brokers was subsequently abandoned, and the schedule revised. The objective of the consolidation is to form a group of well-capitalized universal brokers that can provide efficient and cost-effective intermediation for investors, and are robust enough to withstand the pressures of the stockbroking business. Furthermore, mergers between merchant banks and stockbroking companies or discount houses are to be encouraged, with a view to developing merchant banks into full-fledged investment banks. To facilitate this process, the legal and regulatory framework governing the banking and securities industries (supervised respectively by Bank Negara Malaysia and the Securities Commission) would need to be harmonized.

The Financial Sector Masterplan envisages that a deposit insurance fund be established to replace the current blanket deposit guarantee by the government that has been in place since January 1998. Contributions to the fund would be risk adjusted. Such a premium structure will avoid the moral hazard created by a blanket guarantee and create an incentive for prudent management in line with the move toward performance-based prudential regulation.

The 1999 amendment of the Labuan Offshore Financial Services Authority Act provides the authorities with the power to supervise offshore banking activities in Labuan. The agency is allowed to perform on-site work in the branches where necessary and to require the submission of any information relating to specific activities within its supervisory mandate. The amendment also provides for home country supervisors, including Bank Negara Malaysia, to conduct on-site supervision of their country's branches in Labuan. Beyond supervisory matters, the government's objectives regarding the Labuan Offshore Financial Center include the promotion and diversification of the financial players in the center; the development of Islamic banking; and the development of capital market, e-commerce, and the ancillary activities.

An efficient, progressive, and comprehensive Islamic financial sector is also an element of the long-run vision for Malaysia's financial system. To achieve this, efforts will be needed to enhance institutional capacity, and to develop financial infrastructure and the appropriate regulatory framework. It is envisaged that by 2010, Islamic banking could comprise 20 percent of the banking and insurance market share.

VII   Corporate Performance and Reform

Yougesh Khatri

Corporate sector vulnerabilities and governance issues are increasingly seen to have played key roles in the Asian crisis. Recent economic literature has gone so far as to place these at the center of the crisis. While the debate as to the main causes of the crisis will no doubt continue, it is clearly important to be able to identify the main corporate sector vulnerabilities and to ensure that sufficient reforms are undertaken in order to avoid future crises stemming from the corporate sector and to ensure that this sector can withstand financial crises, whatever the cause.

This section provides a brief overview of the corporate sector in Malaysia; discusses possible links between the corporate sector and the recent crisis; examines corporate performance before, during, and after the crisis; and assesses progress with corporate reform. Various indicators provide evidence of a deterioration in corporate performance before the crisis, a significant negative impact on the sector with the onset of the crisis, and strong signs of recovery in 1999. There is clear evidence of progress with reforms, although this progress has been somewhat uneven: debt restructuring has proceeded well under the Corporate Debt Restructuring Committee and Danaharta; some operational restructuring has taken place through the resolution by Danaharta of its nonperforming loans portfolio; and there have been concerted efforts made to adopt the proposals of the Finance Committee's Report on Corporate Governance. These reforms will take time to complete and become effective, but momentum should not be lost in the face of either an improving or deteriorating environment.

Key Features of the Corporate Sector[1]

The Malaysian corporate sector is large and for most of the last decade has been characterized by rapid growth, mainly driven by increasing stock prices and a high level of new equity issues and privatizations (relative to the region). The Malaysian corporate sector is highly concentrated both in terms of ownership and control. The "insider" system of corporate governance applies and, together with an overreliance on bank financing, the sector has some innate vulnerabilities.

Capital Market Structure

The Malaysian capital market and underlying corporate sector are large by any standard. The total capitalization of the Kuala Lumpur stock exchange, including financial and nonfinancial corporations on the main and second boards, amounted to RM 424 billion ($112 billion) or 125 percent of GDP at end-2000. At its peak in 1993, market capitalization reached 360 percent of GDP. The International Finance Corporation's *Emerging Stock Markets Factbook 1999*, ranked Malaysia's market capitalization at end-1998 as the twenty-third largest in the world; its total value traded was twenty-ninth highest in the world; and, by number of listed companies, Malaysia ranked fifteenth in the world.

The corporate sector was characterized by rapid growth throughout the 1990s. The number of listed companies in Malaysia increased to 795 from 285 in 1990 by the end of the decade (Figure 7.1). The number of listed companies grew on average by 11.6 percent a year throughout the 1990s, and by 14 percent for the period 1990–96. Compared to the other crisis countries, this was relatively rapid: Indonesia averaged a 10 percent annual growth in the number of listed companies throughout the decade, but that was from a much lower base (122 in 1990); Korea averaged only 1 percent annual growth, but from a much higher base (669 listed companies in 1990);[2] Thailand averaged over 7 percent annually for the decade, but 13.6 percent in

---

[1]See also Kochhar and others (1999), Chapter IV.

[2]The number of firms listed on the Korean stock exchange and its overall capitalization may be misleading as the KOSDAQ (similar to the NASDAQ in the United States) has been growing rapidly, and this growth is not reflected by the stock exchange figures.

Figure 7.1. Selected Asian Countries: Capital Market Overview

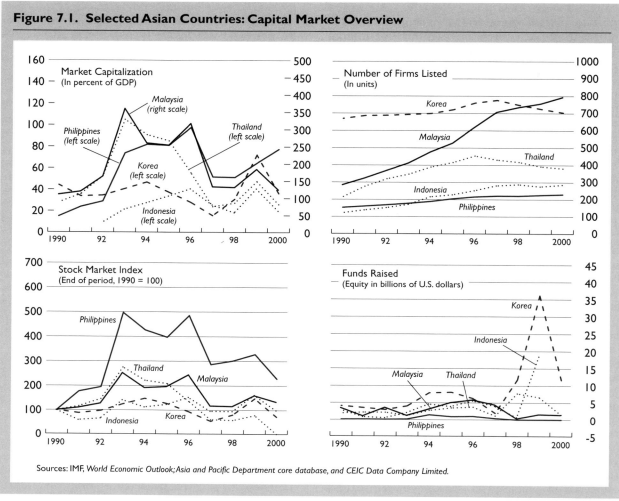

Sources: IMF, *World Economic Outlook; Asia and Pacific Department core database,* and CEIC Data Company Limited.

the 1990–96 period. Market capitalization in Malaysia grew by an average rate of over 40 percent in the 1990–96 period and by an average of nearly 30 percent for the decade. This was not unusual for the region; Indonesia and the Philippines had more rapid growth rates but from a much lower base.

The growth in market capitalization in Malaysia was driven mainly by increases in stock prices, but also by new equity issues and privatization. Stock prices increased by a factor of over 2.4 between 1990 and 1996, and by a factor of 5 for the Philippines, compared to between 1 and 1.5 for the other crisis countries. In the precrisis period, only Korea raised more funds through the equity market in absolute terms than Malaysia. Malaysia was at the forefront of Asian privatization, and Malaysian privatizations, which accounted for a large portion of total new equity raised in the country, also constituted around one-third of total revenue from

privatization in the region (Harvey and Roper, 1999).[3]

While the amount of new equity raised was large by regional comparison, Malaysia was still highly dependent on bank financing. New financial flows to corporations in the period prior to the crisis (1995–97) were mainly from the domestic banking system, representing nearly 60 percent of net funds compared to around 15 percent from equity, 11 percent from domestic debt markets, and 16 percent raised through external borrowing (World Bank, 1999a). The authorities, however, are attempting to develop the domestic bond market and are encouraging corporations to diversify their sources of funding.

---

[3]In early 1991, Malaysia released its privatization master plan, which had the objective of privatizing key industries, and proceeded with Tenaga Nasional, the national electricity company—one of the largest privatizations to date in Asia at $1.2 billion. Between 1992 and 1995, privatization revenue averaged 3 percent of annual GDP.

Box 7.1. The Insider and Outsider Systems of Corporate Governance

Corporate governance relates to ways in which investors and owners (principals) oversee managers who run the firms (agents). There are essentially two main systems of corporate governance, referred to as the insider and outsider systems.

The outsider system refers to the Anglo-American system where typically ownership of firms is widely dispersed and control is delegated to professional managers; the number of listed companies is large; the process of acquiring control is market oriented (i.e., there is a liquid capital market with frequently traded ownership and control rights); there are few interlocked patterns of ownership; and there are few major controlling shareholders, which are rarely associated with the corporate sector itself.

The insider system is characterized by the following features: there is a high concentration of ownership; the corporate sector has controlling interests in itself; the number of listed companies is relatively small; the capital market is illiquid because controlling blocks are held by a few major shareholders, and these are held rather than traded; there are a large number of holding or interlocked companies acting to deter outsiders from acquiring control; and major shareholders typically

also play an active role in management and have the decisive vote in major decisions.

To illustrate the contrast between the outsider (mainly the United Kingdom and the United States) and insider systems (most other countries, including continental Europe and Asia), Crama and others (1999) find that the largest owner in the median U.K.-listed company in 1998 had a stake of less than 15 percent, and less than 5 percent in the median U.S.-listed company; compared with over 80 percent of listed nonfinancial companies in continental Europe that had shareholders with a blocking minority (at least 25 percent) and where around half the companies had one shareholder with an absolute majority. La Porta, Lopez-de-Silanes, and Shleifer (1998) find the average share of common stock owned by the largest three shareholders in the largest companies to be 54 percent in Malaysia, 46 percent in Thailand, 20 percent in Korea, and 18 percent in Japan, compared to less than 15 percent in the United Kingdom and the United States.

Both systems have relative strengths and weaknesses that are typically analyzed in a principal-agent framework. Some of the main issues are summarized below (mainly from Crama and others, 1999).

Ownership and Voting Power: Structures and Consequences

A: Dispersed ownership and dispersed voting power
(United Kingdom, United States)

Advantages: Portfolio diversification and liquidity; takeover possibility

Disadvantages: Insufficient monitoring and free-riding problem

Agency conflicts: Management vs. shareholders

B: Dispersed ownership and concentrated voting power
(Countries where a stake holder can collect proxy votes and shareholder coalitions are allowed)

Advantages: Portfolio diversification and liquidity; monitoring of management

Disadvantages: Violation of one-share-one-vote principle; reduced takeover possibility

Agency conflicts: Controlling block holders vs. small shareholders

C: Concentrated ownership and dispersed voting power
(Any company with voting right restrictions)

Advantages: Protection of minority holders' rights

Disadvantages: Violation of one-share-one-vote principle; low monitoring incentives; low portfolio diversification possibilities; low liquidity; higher cost of capital; reduced takeover possibilities

Agency conflicts: Management vs. shareholders

D: Concentrated ownership and concentrated voting power
(continental Europe, Asia, and any company after a takeover)

Advantages: High monitoring incentives; more focused strategic direction, restructuring, and long-term commitment

Disadvantages: Low portfolio diversification possibilities; low liquidity; reduced takeover possibilities

Agency conflicts: Controlling block holders vs. small shareholders

The Asian crisis economies (which fall under Type D) are characterized by highly concentrated ownership and control, and thus the classic agency problem (between management and shareholders) becomes irrelevant. Another agency conflict arises, however, between insiders (major shareholders) and outsiders (small shareholders), and the main problem of corporate governance becomes how to ensure that the insiders do not exploit (expropriate) the assets of outsiders.

Table 7.1. A Comparison of Legal Protection, Accounting Standards, Institutions, and Enforcement in Various Countries

	Shareholder Protection[1]	Creditor Protection[1]	Degree of Judicial Enforcement[2]	Accounting Standards[3]
Malaysia	3.0	4	7.7	76
Korea	2.0	3	6.7	62
Thailand	3.0	3	5.9	64
Latin America[4]	2.5	1	6.2	53
United States	5.0	1	9.5	71
United Kingdom	4.0	4	9.4	78
Japan	3.0	2	9.4	65
Germany	1.0	4	9.4	62

Source: La Porta, Lopez-de-Silanes, and Shleifer (1998).
[1]On a scale from 1 (weakest) to 5 (strongest).
[2]On a scale from 1 (lowest) to 10 (highest).
[3]The higher the measure, the higher the standard.
[4]Average of Argentina, Brazil, Chile, and Mexico.

Malaysia, like the other crisis countries, is characterized by the insider system of corporate governance (Box 7.1), in which there is a high degree of ownership concentration, cross holdings, and participation of owners in management. A few large corporations account for a significant proportion of financial assets and productive capacity in the country.[4] Concentration also occurs at the level of stock ownership, which, given the large capitalization, is in the hands of relatively few institutional and corporate investors. Another layer of concentration occurs in terms of control, where "pyramiding" or cross-holding of share ownership magnifies the actual control of a few individuals or entities well beyond their actual level of ownership in each company.

The development path of the corporate sector has resulted in some innate vulnerabilities. First, the development of the private sector under the activist industrial policies of the government has resulted in close ties between government and large corporations. Second, the cross-holding structures can create incentives for double leveraging and thus create a multiplier effect in the sensitivity of corporate wealth to changes in the equity market (Kochhar and others, 1999, Chapter IV). Third, the

concentration of shareholding can lead to poor governance because a small group can exercise control over a firm and pursue the objectives of the insiders at the cost of the outsiders or small shareholders (Claessens, Djankov, and Lang, 1999; and Box 7.1). An interesting feature of corporate ownership in Malaysia was the prevalence of nominee accounts. Nominee accounts at end-1997 were the largest type of shareholders in the top five shareholders of listed companies, and about half the beneficial owners of the nominee accounts were foreigners. A recently issued set of rules by the Kuala Lumpur stock exchange requiring securities accounts to be opened in the name of the beneficial owner means that nominee accounts can be expected to be phased out soon.

Legal and Institutional Structure

The nonfinancial corporate sector in Malaysia is mainly governed by three acts: the Companies Act, 1965; the Securities Industry Act, 1983; and the Securities Commission Act, 1993.[5] The Kuala Lumpur stock exchange's listing requirements and rules also play an important role in regulating investors, brokers,

---

[4]The International Finance Corporation produces an indicator of this type of concentration derived from the ten largest stocks in the IFC global indices for each country relative to the total International Finance Corporation Global market capitalization for each country. At end-1998, this measure of concentration was 31.5 percent for Malaysia compared with 61.5 percent for Indonesia, 37.9 percent for Korea, 55.4 percent for the Philippines, and 45.8 percent for Thailand.

[5]Also relevant to the financial corporations and the broader legal and institutional environment in which corporations operate are: the Futures Industry Act of 1993, the Banking and Financial Institutions Act of 1989, and the Malaysian Code on Takeovers and Mergers of 1987, all of which were supplemented by guidelines such as those of the Kuala Lumpur stock exchange (mentioned above) and the Foreign Investment Committee.

and issuers. The Companies Act deals with the pre-incorporation, incorporation, operations, and duties of companies and their directors, as well as the rights and obligations of shareholders and directors. The Securities Industry Act and Securities Commission Act make up the legislative and regulatory frameworks of Malaysia's capital markets, under the authority of the Ministry of Finance. The powers of the Kuala Lumpur stock exchange were recently strengthened through amendments to the Securities Industry Act, such that the exchange may now take action against directors and any person involved with its listing requirements.[6]

Malaysia has comprehensive laws relating to corporate governance, and the laws governing creditor rights are comparable to those of OECD countries (Table 7.1). While accounting standards are also good, enforcement and actual practice have been weaker. The Financial Reporting Act of 1997 was designed to address this issue by giving the force of law to (i.e., requiring all companies to comply with) the accounting standards approved by the national accounting body, the Malaysian Accounting Standards Board. Most of the accounting standards approved by this board are based on international accounting standards. While progress with improving standards and adopting international best practices has been notable, the accuracy of financial data needs to be improved by bringing financial disclosure requirements in line with international best practices. The broader legal and institutional environment is strong, although transparency and accountability in the public sector need more attention (World Bank, 1999b).

There are a number of alternatives for dealing with distressed corporations. The Companies Act allows creditors to petition the high courts to wind up a company if that company defaults on debt payments, and allows debtors to petition for court protection under Section 176 until a group of creditors (representing three-fourths of the outstanding debt) agree to a reorganization plan.[7] Companies and creditors can also opt for voluntary out-of-court restructuring of the debt or, for companies with debt exceeding RM 50 million and having more than three creditors, the voluntary out-of-court restructuring can be done through the Corporate Debt Restructuring Committee.[8]

Corporate Sector and Financial Crises

There are two main branches of economic literature that link the corporate sector with financial crises. The main literature on crises has been at the macroeconomic level focusing on macroeconomic fundamentals or self-fulfilling crises (modeled on bank runs), and has only recently (in a model by Krugman) included explicitly the corporate sector as a central element. The other branch of the literature is more microeconomic based, looking at either firm-level data to investigate the role of the corporate sector in the crisis or focusing on the role of institutional factors and corporate governance.

Macroeconomic Approaches

Standard Models of Financial Crises

The literature on financial crises has a long history and extends well beyond the scope of this section.[9] The main prevailing theories have been classified by Eichengreen as "first generation" and "second generation" models. First generation models are associated with the seminal paper by Krugman (1992) and generally explain crises as a result of a deterioration in fundamentals. The main feature of second generation models (following Obstfeld, 1986) is self-fulfilling speculative attacks, although even for these some perceived weakness in fundamentals seems to be the key trigger for the speculative attack.[10] The development of the second generation models followed the breakdown of the exchange rate mechanism in 1993 and the Mexican crisis in 1994, as aspects of these crises were hard to reconcile with the first generation models. This was mainly because the decisions to abandon pegs were not related to the exhaustion of reserves in defending the currency and, in some cases, were not easily explicable at all from the point of view of economic fundamentals.

The Asian crisis seemed to consolidate the consensus toward the second generation models as representing more recent crises. Krugman (1999) suggests, however, that for the major crises in the Asian countries, neither of these models seems to have

---

[6]For more details on the legal and institutional environment governing corporations, see the forthcoming publication, *Malaysia: Corporate Governance Assessment* by the World Bank.

[7]In response to certain weaknesses identified in the Companies Act, key provisions of Section 176 were tightened after the onset of the crisis in an attempt to prevent misuse of the Act as a means to delay adjustment.

[8]For a fuller discussion of the problems with enforcement of laws, autonomy of regulators, transparency in exercising existing regulation, and confusion over jurisdictional boundaries, see Kochhar and others (1999), Chapter IV.

[9]See, for example, the survey in Berg and others (1999) and the references therein.

[10]A crude caricature of the first generation model is one in which a budget deficit is financed by "printing money," which results in the eventual collapse of a fixed exchange rate. In second generation models, the crisis results from a conflict between a fixed exchange rate regime and the desire to pursue a more expansionary monetary policy; investors bet that the authorities will let the peg go rather than compromise on another front, such as employment, and this bet is self-fulfilling.

much relevance.[11] The fiscal positions, by conventional measures, were strong, and there were not really the clear trade-offs between employment and exchange rate stability (e.g., as faced by the United Kingdom in 1992). Krugman suggests the need for a "third generation" of crisis models and is skeptical about the current bank-centered candidates (Corsetti, Pesenti, and Roubini, 1998; or Chang and Velasco, 1998).[12] Krugman acknowledges that these models capture some aspects of the crisis, but outlines an alternative candidate that emphasizes factors not formally included in previous models, namely, the role of companies' balance sheets in determining their ability to invest and the role of capital flows in affecting real exchange rates.

Krugman's Proposed Third Generation Model

Reliance on the moral hazard argument, according to Corsetti, Pesenti, and Roubini, is discounted as a key feature by Krugman, who argues that there was ample evidence of significant investment in the Asian crisis countries prior to the crisis, including in direct foreign purchases of equity and real estate, which clearly were not protected by any form of implicit guarantee. Krugman does, however, accept the existence of multiple equilibria as a necessary element in modeling the crisis, although not the mechanism implicit in the Diamond-Dybvig type approach. The Krugman model incorporates three key elements:

- contagion;

- the transfer problem:[13] A huge change is needed in the current account as a counterpart to the reversal in capital flows, which is evidently central to the crisis yet has not been explicitly included in previous models; and

- balance sheet problems: Most descriptive accounts of the crisis place significant emphasis on the role of firms' balance sheets, but this had not been featured as a central element in the crisis literature.[14]

The model is characterized by multiple equilibria, where a loss of confidence, for whatever reason, can lead to a self-fulfilling collapse; the mechanism differs from the Diamond-Dybvig approach in that the main mechanism is the transfer problem. Very roughly speaking, the loss of confidence leads to the transfer problem, and to achieve the required current account reversal, the country must experience a large real depreciation and/or output decline, either of which adversely affects the balance sheets of domestic firms. This validates the initial loss of confidence, i.e., moving from the high expected investment equilibrium to the low expected investment equilibrium. According to the model, the factors that make such a crisis possible (i.e., reinforce the feedback loop between investment, real exchange rates, and balance sheets) are high leverage, low marginal propensity to import, and large foreign currency debt relative to exports.

Microeconomic and Institutional Approaches

A number of studies have used firm level data to investigate (in a comparative context) the corporate performance of the crisis countries during the 1990s, including Claessens, Djankov, and Lang (1998), Pomerleano (1998), Harvey and Roper (1999), and Claessens, Djankov, and Xu (2000). These studies provide new evidence suggesting that the causes of the Asian crisis may lie in firm-based decisions.

Claessens, Djankov, and Xu summarize the literature on the role of the corporate sector, in both performance and financing, in the Asian crisis and identify four main possible links, summarized briefly below.

First, the weak corporate performance after the crisis was related largely to the shocks experienced by the Asian countries, including declines in aggregate demand, reversal of capital flows, sharp depreciations, and increases in interest rates (Furman and Stiglitz, 1998). As yet, there is little empirical work assessing the importance of aggregate shocks to corporate performance. There is some evidence from

---

[11]Note that Krugman (1999) has a somewhat different view from that of Krugman (1998).

[12]Two major views have emerged in the postcrisis literature. The first view (Corsetti, Pesenti, and Roubini, 1998) suggests that the apparent soundness of macroeconomic policy was misleading because a large hidden subsidy via implicit government guarantees to banks and corporations led to moral-hazard lending and implied a hidden government deficit. Thus the apparent soundness of the macroeconomic policy was an illusion. The second view, associated with Radelet and Sachs (1998), may be characterized by the idea that there was not a major problem with the policies pursued by the crisis countries and that investments were basically sound; at most, the countries suffered from "financial fragility" and were thus vulnerable to self-fulfilling pessimism on the part of international lenders (see models by Chang and Velasco, 1998).

[13]The transfer problem—discussed by Keynes, among others—refers to the difficulty in transferring large quantities of capital from one country to other countries. The problem relates to the burden of making the transfer, but also to the burden associated with the resultant change in exchange rates and relative prices.

---

[14]The role of firms' balance sheets in the crisis has most often been related to the impact of massive exchange rate depreciations on the domestic value of the foreign currency–denominated debt of these firms, which had been accumulating prior to the crisis. Balance sheets were further weakened by declining sales and high interest rates. These problems in turn led to the increase in nonperforming loans, but this view implies that the problem was not, per se, a banking system problem.

survey data, such as the results of a survey of Thai industrial firms reported in Dollar and Hallward-Driemeier (2000),[15] that indicates these shocks played an important but not exclusive role in the performance of these firms during the crisis.

Second, the poor performance of the corporate sectors during and after the crisis reflects previous fundamental weaknesses (Corsetti, Pesenti, and Roubini, 1998). This view implies that the performance of firms was not adequately monitored by shareholders and investors, and/or firms were not subject to sufficient competition, thus poor performers or riskier firms were not forced to fully adjust and increase their rates of return to compensate investors for higher risk. This view may also imply that profitability was overstated by firms: thus the lack of transparency, relatively weak accounting practices in the region, and weak corporate governance may have hidden the extent of the problems and delayed the onset of the crisis.[16] A number of studies indicate that ownership structure may induce risky behavior. The insider system (Box 7.1) prevails in the Asian countries: the extensive links and cross-holdings of shares, particularly between corporations and banks, are likely to have distorted the market allocation of resources and resulted in excessive and nontransparent risk. These ownership links clearly played a significant role in Korea and Indonesia. Government involvement—through direct participation in bank ownership and through links with corporations and banks—is also likely to weaken the allocation of resources because a political dimension is introduced into the allocation decisions.

Third, aggregate and financial shocks to the financial sector may result in a credit crunch, constraining lending to viable corporations with profitable investment and trading opportunities. Shocks—financial, real, or regulatory—may cause a real or perceived shortage of capital for banks and lead to their curtailing credit for investment or trade, thus impairing the performance of firms. A credit crunch may result from weak financial institutions or from a change in the regulatory and supervisory environment. Increased uncertainty regarding whether and at what price loans will be available may also result in a shortfall of loanable funds (Stiglitz and Weiss,

1981). The balance sheet problem (Bernake and Gertler, 1995) may exacerbate the effect of a shock: in the presence of asymmetric information and principal-agent relationships, the corporation's net worth or wealth becomes an important determinant of the amount it can borrow, as assumed in the Krugman model, rather than the prospects of the project for which the borrowing is undertaken. Thus, a decline in the wealth of a firm (e.g., through depreciation that reduces the domestic value of foreign assets) can reduce the credit available even for viable new projects.

Fourth, the efficiency of debt-resolution mechanisms will determine, in part, the extent of the impact of financial and other shocks. It has long been recognized that the institutional framework is important in avoiding and resolving systemic financial crises and that exceptional mechanisms, such as Fund programs, may be required during periods of systemic crisis. This broad area of literature spans economic principles for optimal workouts to the importance of creditor rights to enforce claims and seize collateral, both in the context of domestic and external borrowing, as seen in the review by La Porta, Lopez-de-Silanes, and Shleifer (1999).

Corporate Performance

Financial ratios, which are commonly used to analyze corporate performance, have the advantage of being simple to compile and are broadly understood, but they have some major drawbacks. Simple financial ratios generally give a partial indication of performance in a particular dimension. Financial ratios can also be misleading (e.g., looking at rates of returns rather than risk-adjusted rates of return). Economic measures based on concepts of efficiency—measured relative to other firms—or total factor productivity—measured for a firm over time—provide more comprehensive measures of performance, but require detailed production (input-output) data. Generally, only accounting data are readily available on a consistent basis between firms and over time, and thus an analysis of corporate performance has generally employed a financial ratio analysis.

Below, performance is analyzed based on financial ratios, but also on approximations to the economic measures of efficiency and productivity using accounting data. This provides evidence that performance in the Malaysian corporate sector, and in the corporate sector of the other crisis countries, deteriorated prior to the crisis, but deteriorated even more dramatically with the onset of the crisis. The evidence is consistent with a number of the possible links identified above, although no formal tests were conducted.

---

[15]The survey found that 60 percent of firms said that the substantial decline in domestic demand and higher input costs relating to the depreciation were the primary sources of difficulty. Only one-third of the firms cited access to capital as a major problem, although more cited the cost of capital as a problem.

[16]Weak corporate governance and a lack of transparency are the central factors in explaining the Asian crisis according to Johnson and others (1998). But, as Furman and Stiglitz (1998) point out, countries with few problems in terms of corporate governance and transparency have still experienced crises (e.g., Sweden).

Table 7.2. Financial Ratios for Listed Nonfinancial Companies in Malaysia
(In percent, unless otherwise indicated)

	1995	1996	1997	1998	1999
Profit (after tax)/Turnover (net profit margin)	10.5	10.1	7.5	−3.7	−1.1
Return on shareholder's funds	11.0	10.8	7.6	−4.9	−2.4
Return on assets	5.3	4.6	2.9	−1.8	−0.8
Earnings yield (equals 1/Net price-earnings ratio)	4.3	3.9	4.2	−4.4	−1.6
Net dividend yield	1.5	1.1	1.5	2.1	1.8
Current ratio (equals current assets/current liabilities)	1.2	1.1	1.1	1.0	1.0
Total debt-to-equity ratio	0.5	0.7	0.9	1.0	1.1
Number of companies included in calculating these ratios	473	541	627	664	325

Source: Kuala Lumpur stock exchange data provided in April 2000.

Financial Indicators of Corporate Performance and Risk

Performance, as measured by the net profit margin, seemed relatively healthy in Malaysia and did not appear to diminish markedly before the crisis (Table 7.2). The net profit margin compared favorably with those of the other crisis countries, and prior to the crisis was only surpassed by that of Indonesia (Table 7.3).[17] Unlike the other crisis countries, the Malaysian corporate sector in aggregate was still profitable in 1997; thus, Malaysia appears to have entered the crisis later or fared better going into it. There were, however, signs of increasing corporate distress going into the crisis, as indicated by the percentage of firms not able to cover interest expenses from operational cash flows.

While Malaysia appears to have fared comparably well going into the crisis, it did no better than the other countries during the crisis or the recovery period. Lack of a differentially superior postcrisis performance, given the more favorable starting conditions, may reflect either the lag with which the crisis affected Malaysia or the later pickup in domestic demand compared with the other countries (see Section II). Also, because Malaysia has a significantly larger market capitalization relative to GDP, the stock market declines during the crisis are likely to have resulted in a larger loss of wealth and

an increase in leverage, thus enhancing corporate stress. An alternative explanation is suggested below (see Corporate Performance and Links to the Crisis).

An alternative measure of corporate performance is the return on assets, which has the advantage of not being affected by the liability structure of a firm while providing a measure of return on capital.[18] The return on assets in Malaysia tell a similar story to net profit margins, although there is a more obvious decline in the return on assets just prior to the crisis (Table 7.2). Claessens, Djankov, and Xu (2000) compare real return on assets, which they define as return on assets less the inflation rate, in a sample of Asian countries and the United States and Germany. The findings reveal that the average real return on assets for the precrisis period of 1988–96 in Thailand, the Philippines, and Indonesia were the highest among the sample of 36 countries (that report to Worldscope) at 9.8 percent, 7.9 percent, and 7.1 percent, respectively. Malaysia's average for the same period was not far behind at 6.3 percent—ranking eighth in the sample of 36—and greater than that of either the United States (5.3 percent) or Germany (4.7 percent). Korea had one of the lowest real return on assets for the period in the sample at 3.7 percent. Indonesia, Thailand, and Korea had declining trends in real return on assets between 1990 and 1996, with Korea measured from an already low base, while Malaysia had an increasing trend between 1988 and 1993, but a declining one there-

---

[17]The net profit margin reported by Claessens, Djankov, and Lang (1999) in this table differs from that derived using the Kuala Lumpur stock exchange data in Table 7.2. This may be due to a different sample (Table 7.2 is limited to nonfinancial corporations) or different definitions. Also, the net profit margin in Table 7.2 is defined as earnings before interest and tax less tax relative to turnover.

[18]The return on assets is nevertheless a partial measure of performance because it only takes into account returns with respect to capital and not other factors, such as labor.

Table 7.3. Operational Performance of Publicly Traded Corporations and Share of Distressed Corporations in Selected Asian Countries
(In percent)

	1995	1996	1997	1998	1999 (First half)
Net profit margin					
Indonesia	12.4	13.9	−3.6	−13.3	−8.9
Korea	2.7	0.4	−0.3	−2.6	2.7
Malaysia	12.2	12.0	6.9	−2.8	1.3
Thailand	7.1	5.1	−3.6	2.2	4.8
Firms unable to cover interest expenses from operational cash flows					
Indonesia	12.6	17.9	40.3	58.2	63.8
Korea	8.5	11.2	24.3	33.8	26.7
Malaysia	3.4	5.6	17.1	34.3	26.3
Thailand	6.7	10.4	32.6	30.4	28.3

Source: Claessens, Djankov, and Klingebiel (1999).

Table 7.4. Debt/Equity Ratios in Selected Economies
(In percent)

	1990	1991	1992	1993	1994	1995	1996
Hong Kong SAR	1.8	2.0	1.8	1.8	2.3	2.0	1.6
Indonesia	—	1.9	2.1	2.1	1.7	2.1	1.9
Japan	2.9	2.0	2.0	2.1	2.2	2.4	2.4
Korea	3.1	3.2	3.4	3.6	3.5	3.8	3.5
Malaysia	1.0	0.6	0.6	0.7	1.0	1.0	1.2
Philippines	—	0.8	1.2	1.2	1.1	1.2	1.3
Singapore	0.9	0.9	0.9	1.1	0.9	1.0	1.0
Taiwan Province of China	—	0.7	0.9	0.9	0.9	0.8	0.8
Thailand	2.2	2.0	1.8	1.9	2.1	2.2	2.4
Germany	1.6	1.6	1.5	1.5	1.5	1.5	1.5
United States	0.9	1.0	1.1	1.1	1.1	1.1	1.1

Source: Claessens, Djankov, and Xu (2000).

after through 1996. Thus, return on assets—measured in real terms and over a longer period—seems to indicate declining corporate performance in the precrisis period.

A number of risk indicators worsened prior to the crisis. Measures such as the proportion of distressed corporates (Table 7.3), leverage (Table 7.4), and the maturity structure of debt clearly indicate that risk was increasing in the run-up to the crisis.[19] Higher

returns would normally be required to justify this increased risk. In effect, accounting returns, although generally high, were declining, and implicit risk-adjusted returns were declining even more rapidly.

---

[19]The ratio of long-term debt to total debt was relatively low in the region and declined steadily in Malaysia to average less than one-third for the period 1988–96. The ratios for the same period were 34.1 percent in Indonesia, 43.7 percent in Korea, 52.2 percent in the Philippines, and 30.9 percent in Thailand. These are low compared to the average U.S. and German long-term-to-total debt ratios for the same period: 55.3 percent for Germany and 75.9 percent for the United States (Claessens, Djankov, and Xu, 2000).

Table 7.5. A Comparison of Stock Market Returns and Risk in Selected Economies
(During period of January 1990–December 1996)

	Buy and Hold	Average Annualized Monthly Return	Annualized Standard Deviation
Indonesia	11.10	3.09	103.55
Korea	–47.33	–9.52	95.47
Malaysia	127.13	11.80	85.02
Philippines	118.13	9.55	109.07
Taiwan Province of China	–42.89	–4.26	151.92
Thailand	29.56	3.12	111.48
United States	184.14	13.96	39.76
World	78.55	7.60	46.20

Source: Harvey and Roper, 1999.

Summary statistics on the distribution of firm-level indicators of nonfinancial corporate performance reported by Harvey and Roper also suggest that corporate performance in the Asian countries—but also in other emerging markets—deteriorated in the run-up to the Asian crisis. Harvey and Roper report statistics on the entire distribution of returns on equity and returns on invested capital from firm-level ratios for a number of emerging markets. They determine that the median of these indicators had clearly declined in Indonesia and Thailand, and less clearly so in Korea, the Philippines, and Malaysia.[20] More generally, the reported medians of a series of corporate performance indicators—namely return on equity, return on invested capital, total debt-to-common equity, and interest payments relative to earnings before interest and tax—show a deterioration in the main Asian and Latin American emerging markets between 1992 and 1996, with the clear exception of Mexico, for which three out of four indicators improved.

A related form of return measure is that on stock market investment. Harvey and Roper estimate the buy-and-hold returns accruing to investors between January 1990 and December 1996 for various countries and conclude that returns in the Asian crisis countries declined prior to the crisis and that risk-adjusted returns were relatively poor in Asia. Only Malaysia and the Philippines outperformed the World Morgan Stanley Capital Index over the pe-

riod, while the U.S. Morgan Stanley Capital Index had both a higher return and lower volatility (or risk) than all of the Asian countries (Table 7.5). Throughout Asia, Harvey and Roper also find that returns in individual markets deteriorated well before the onset of the crisis. Although the buy-and-hold investment strategy is a naïve one, after considering alternative dynamic strategies Harvey and Roper still find that Asian returns failed to outperform either U.S. or world dynamic strategies.

A popular measure of liquidity, the current ratio (see Table 7.2) indicates that liquidity in Malaysia's corporate sector declined slightly before and during the crisis. Negative profits during and immediately after the crisis imply that cash reserves and other liquid assets likely had declined. New borrowing for investment declined significantly with the onset of the crisis, and new investment was partly financed from retained earnings, further decreasing current assets relative to current liabilities.

Leverage in the corporate sector, measured as the ratio of total debt to equity, was rising rapidly in Malaysia in the precrisis period, but has since stabilized (Table 2.1 and Table 7.5). Harvey and Roper note that the entire distribution of leverage ratios at the firm level shifted right or worsened between 1992 and 1996. Reporting the distribution by quartiles, they find that in 1992, a quarter of the firms had leveraged 2.1 percent of the common stock, half had reported a leverage ratio of 18.9 percent or less, and three-quarters of the firms had stated their leverage ratio was less than 50 percent. By 1996, the corresponding values for the first, second, and third quartiles had increased to 12 percent, 58 percent, and 112 percent, respectively.

---

[20]For Indonesia, the median return on equity declined to 12.5 percent in 1996 from 15 percent in 1992, while for Thailand, it declined more markedly to 7.7 percent from 19.4 percent over the same period.

Economic Measures of Corporate Performance

Efficiency and productivity are the main economic measures of performance. Technically efficient firms use the least combinations of inputs, such as labor and capital, to produce a unit of output at a given point in time and for a given environment, such as technological and institutional infrastructure. The firms using the least inputs to produce output define the production frontier, which relates output to inputs, or, equivalently, the efficient unit isoquant, the efficient input combinations that can produce one unit of output. Firms not on the production frontier (i.e., not on the unit isoquant) are said to be inefficient; the level of inefficiency can be measured by the "distance" from the frontier.[21] Shifts in the production frontier—and, correspondingly, the unit isoquant—can be thought of as technological change but will generally reflect changes in the exogenous environment in the broad sense of all factors exogenous to the firm. Total factor productivity conflates efficiency changes with technological change and broader changes in the exogenous environment and is thus a residual catch-all measure.

Ideally, to calculate efficiency economic measures of inputs and outputs would be used, but as these are not available accounting data are used as proxies. Crude approximations of output (using total sales or turnover), capital (using total assets), and labor and other inputs (using total expenses = turnover – earnings before interest and tax) are derived from the published balance sheets and income statements for the 29 largest nonfinancial corporates for the period 1995–99.[22] Dividing the two input measures (total assets and total expenses) by output (turnover or total revenue), a scatter plot can be derived of the input combinations, of which the lower boundary formed by the points furthest south and/or west is indicative of a unit isoquant. The larger the scatter, the less the implied relative efficiency, and thus the scatter plots for the 1995–99 period (Figure 7.2) indicate a worsening of relative efficiency for these large corporations between 1995 and 1998, but it is unclear from the scatter plots whether efficiency improves or worsens in 1999.

The Malmquist index[23] (Malmquist, 1953; and Fare, Grosskopf, and Lovell, 1994) allows us to jointly derive measures of technical efficiency (distance from the frontier) and exogenous change (i.e., shifts of the frontier that are often attributed to technological change) (Figure 7.3). The derived indices of technical efficiency and exogenous change, using the 29 firms for which 1999 data were already available, indicate that average efficiency declined during 1995–99, while exogenous factors, such as technological change, institutional and regulatory factors, and macroeconomic and international variables, deteriorated somewhat but were strongly positive contributors to total factor productivity in 1999. Figure 7.3 plots chained indexes of changes in average measured efficiency for firms and shifts in the frontier. Bearing in mind the significant reservations with respect to the data expressed earlier, there are indications that technical efficiency and, more strongly, total factor productivity, declined prior to the crisis. This provides further evidence of a deterioration of fundamentals in the corporate sector and in the environment in which corporations operated prior to the crisis. The continued decline in efficiency in 1999 is consistent with the view that the benefits from any restructuring were not likely to be manifested immediately because of transition costs and the dynamics of adjustment. The deterioration in exogenous factors—a shift of the frontier away from the origin—is consistent with the initial deterioration in factors external to the firms, such as increases in interest rates, the large real depreciation, and a decline in aggregate demand, because these will have affected costs for all firms and thus will have shifted the efficient frontier. As these external factors improved, however, it is also possible that the initial pressure to improve efficiency diminished.

The deterioration in corporate sector performance is also evident from the aggregate data on listed nonfinancial corporations. Aggregating total revenue, total assets, and total expenditure for the whole corporate sector in Malaysia (see Table 7.2 for the number of firms included for each year) similar indicators of performance, which combine efficiency and shift in the efficient frontier, can be plotted at an aggregate level over time (Figure 7.4). The aggregate indicators clearly demonstrate a deterioration in the corporate sector's use of total assets (i.e., an increase in the total assets/total revenue ratio) in the run-up to the crisis. In 1997, performance in both dimensions is weaker, and in 1998 a major deterioration occurs in the dimension of expenses relative to revenue, possibly due to a significant shift in the frontier relating to the various exogenous shocks that are discussed further, below.

---

[21]In addition, allocative efficiency requires that the firm not only be on the unit isoquant but also at the point where the budget line or surface determined by the relative input prices is tangential to the unit isoquant.

[22]The Kuala Lumpur stock exchange kindly provided accounting information on the top 40 firms, of which only 29—representing around 40 percent of total market capitalization—had complete accounts through 1999. There are of course significant problems in this analysis, not the least of which are the use of accounting variables as proxies for economic variables, the problem of comparing companies across industries, the aggregation of inputs into only two groups, and the use of only a subset of firms. This analysis should thus be taken as indicative.

---

[23]The Malmquist indices of efficiency and total factor productivity reported here were estimated by Jenifer Piesse of Birkbeck College, University of London.

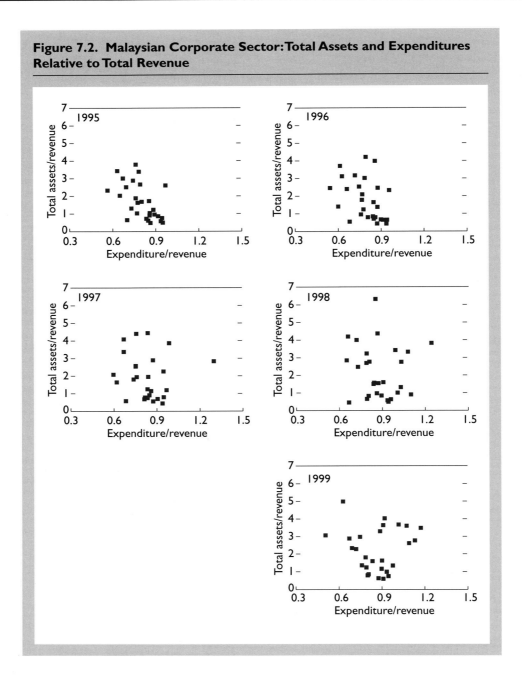

Figure 7.2. Malaysian Corporate Sector: Total Assets and Expenditures Relative to Total Revenue

Corporate Performance and Links to the Crisis

The evidence of deterioration in corporate performance in Malaysia and within the region is consistent with various aspects of the links discussed above. What emerges from the returns measures, particularly when adjusted for risk, and from the economic performance indicators is that performance in the Malaysian corporate sector did indeed deteriorate before the crisis, and there is thus support for the fundamentals-based theories. The evidence, however, is also consistent with Krugman's model if the deterioration in precrisis corporate performance is considered insufficient to have warranted the extent of the crisis. Contagion, together with the deterioration in fundamentals, could have acted as the trigger by causing the change in sentiment that resulted in a shift from high to low equilibrium and ultimately in the full-blown crisis. This view provides

Figure 7.3. Indices of Efficiency, Exogenous Change, and TFP
(1995 = 100)

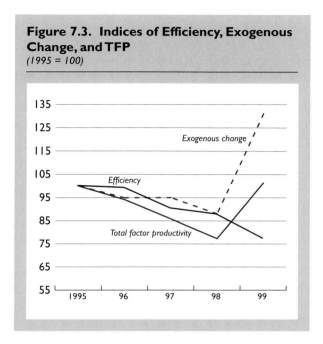

Figure 7.4. Malaysian Corporate Sector: Performance Indicators

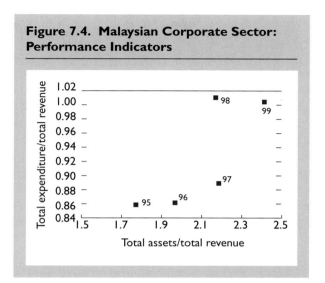

another possible explanation as to why Malaysia went into the crisis in a stronger position and yet, with the onset of the crisis, its performance was similar to the other crisis countries.

Relating to the first link discussed above, associating corporate performance to stocks, there is ample evidence from the accounting and economic measures of corporate performance in Malaysia of a significant deterioration in performance with the onset of the crisis. Measures of net profit margins, return on assets, the number of distressed firms, and firm-level and aggregate efficient measures all deteriorated in 1997 and significantly more so in 1998. The survey evidence in Dollar and Hallward-Driemeier (2000) identifies aggregate shocks as a major, but not the sole cause of the deterioration in performance of manufacturing firms in Thailand. The measure of a shift in the efficient frontier from the Malmquist index provides another indicator of the impact of exogenous factors in explaining a deterioration in corporate performance.

Although not immediately evident from the accounts-based financial ratios, there is evidence of a decline in corporate performance in Malaysia and the other Asian countries before the crisis and thus the second potential link.[24] The accounting measures are only partial indicators and do not adjust for risk. The

evidence indicates that stock market returns in the Asian countries adjusted for risk (volatility) were well below those in other equity markets in the 1990s (Harvey and Roper, 1999); that returns in the Asian stock markets declined well before the onset of the crisis (Harvey and Roper); and that returns on assets were declining in all the crisis countries in the run-up to the crisis, and even more rapidly if adjusted for the increasing risk associated with higher leverage, increasing external debt, and an increasing share of short-term debt. Scatter plots and Malmquist indices show some deterioration in efficiency of the largest Malaysian corporation before the crisis. Thus there is some evidence that appropriate market discipline on firms was missing, but there does not appear to be a problem with misreporting of profitability, and accounting standards appear to be stronger than in other countries in the region. Other factors, such as the ownership structure and government involvement, clearly could also be contributory factors to the increased risk in the corporate sector that did not result in a correspondingly higher required return.

Performance indicators say little about whether or not there has been a credit crunch nor do they indicate whether the real effects of the financial and other shocks were related to the efficiency of debt-resolution mechanisms, the third and fourth possible links. It appears that slow growth in the private sector credit is due to a lack of demand for funds rather than a lack of supply, which is consistent with the overinvestment story (see also Section VI). Ghosh and Ghosh (1999) find that, for Korea and Thailand, the binding constraint was slowing demand rather than an inadequate supply of funds.

With respect to debt resolution, the mechanisms available were inadequate at the onset of the crisis,

---

[24]Of course, this can be considered consistent with the previous link to the extent that there was evidence of a deterioration in corporate performance before the crisis, but the main decline followed the onset of the crisis and the various shocks.

but Malaysia took decisive and effective steps to deal with the emerging problems by creating institutions to deal with nonperforming loans and debt restructuring, as discussed in Section VI and below. Overall, the country has fairly strong legal and institutional frameworks and laws relating to corporate governance, and those governing creditor and shareholder protection are comparable to those of OECD countries (La Porta, Lopez-de-Silanes, and Shleifer, 1998; Table 7.1).

Malaysia is characterized by a high prevalence of collateral-based bank lending, and thus the rapid asset and equity price inflation is likely to have contributed to an increase in bank lending. The roles of contagion, leverage (corporate balance sheets), and the transfer problem are clear in Malaysia, and all of these are central to the Krugman model. The asset price collapse, with the reversal of capital flows and its impact on net wealth, however, was probably a more important factor than the currency depreciation in the feedback loop that resulted in the crisis, but such a collapse is not an explicit part of the Krugman model.[25]

Progress with Corporate Reforms

Corporate reforms can be classified as relating to debt restructuring, operational restructuring, and improvements in corporate governance. The progress achieved by Malaysia with debt restructuring has been significant, and the proactive approach adopted by the authorities seems to have paid off. The extent of progress with operational restructuring is less clear, and the adoption of measures to improve corporate governance will need to be applied evenly before their benefits become apparent.

Debt Restructuring

Debt restructuring in Malaysia has taken a number of forms. The Corporate Debt Restructuring Committee provides a platform—based on London rules—to achieve out-of-court corporate debt restructuring (see Section VI). Restructuring is also occurring on an out-of-court basis and outside of the formal Corporate Debt Restructuring Committee or Danaharta framework. As of end-March 2000, more than 192 companies had filed for court protection under Section 176 of the Companies

Act. Of these, 18 percent of the applications relate to the first quarter of 2000; thus the rate of applications does not appear to be slowing. Firms in the sectors described as finance, insurance, property, or trading have dominated, representing nearly 40 percent of annual, as well as total, applications. Over 1,000 petitions to liquidate companies have been submitted, and there has also been an increase in mergers and acquisitions.[26]

Of the Asian crisis countries, Korea and Malaysia have made the most progress in restructuring debt, achieved mainly out of court. By August 1999, the two countries had completed restructuring of about one-third of the debt registered under their respective programs.

Operational Restructuring

Operational restructuring of Malaysian corporations has proceeded partly through the resolution by Danaharta of its acquired nonperforming loans accomplished by rehabilitation of businesses and liquidation and foreclosure of collateral, and through the elimination of noncore businesses as part of debt-restructuring agreements coordinated by the Corporation Debt Restructuring Committee. By end-2000, Danaharta had appointed special administrators to oversee the management of more than 80 companies under its control to assist in their stabilization and restructuring.

Another important aspect of operational restructuring in the crisis countries has been reductions in labor, which have been the main source of improvement in operational cash flows (Claessens, Djankov, and Klingebiel, 1999). Average labor shedding in publicly listed companies resulted in a 34 percent decrease in payrolls in mid-1999 compared to mid-1997 for Korea, a 12 percent decrease for Thailand, but only a 7 percent decrease for Malaysia. The use of foreign workers in the latter meant that, although there was evidence of labor hoarding (Bank Negara Malaysia, 1999), the flexibility to dismiss foreign workers helped to cushion the domestic labor force from the full impact of the crisis.

Corporate Governance

Significant progress has been made in implementing the recommendations of the Finance Committee's Report on Corporate Governance. The re-

---

[25]Kochhar and others (1999) estimate a relative wealth shock due to changes in the stock market capitalization in Malaysia during the financial crisis, of 155 percent of GDP, compared to the impact on net wealth of the exchange rate depreciation (at its peak) of only 14 percent of GDP.

[26]The number of company liquidations increased from 681 in 1996 to 1,898 in 1997 (an increase of 179 percent) and to 4,800 in 1998 (an increase of 152 percent). Comparing liquidations between January and September 1999 of 3,778, with those between January and September 1998 of 3,438, we see a much smaller increase.

port was made public in March 1999, and the Finance Committee established an Implementation Project Team, consisting of the Ministry of Finance, the Securities Commission, the Registry of Companies, the Kuala Lumpur stock exchange, the Federation of Public Limited Companies, Bank Negara Malaysia, and Malaysian Exchange of Securities Dealing and Automated Quotation. Implementation of the recommendations is taking the form of updating of laws, regulations, and rules in line with international best practices; amendments to the listing requirements of the Kuala Lumpur stock exchange; and development of accreditation programs for existing directors of listed companies. Malaysia also led the Asia-Pacific Economic Cooperation (APEC) finance ministers' initiative on corporate governance; in May 1999, a report was submitted to the APEC finance ministers entitled "Strengthening Corporate Governance in the APEC Region." Most recently, a monitoring body on corporate governance was set up, the Minority Shareholders Watchdog Group, to monitor corporations, provide advice on best practices, and eventually to offer other services like proxy voting. While there has been a concerted effort to improve the corporate governance environment, a few high-profile cases of poor governance relating to companies with political links have undermined market sentiment. Thus it will be important to apply the new code of governance evenly.

Summary and Conclusions

The analysis indicates that corporate performance in Malaysia deteriorated notably prior to the crisis and recovered somewhat in 1999. Some accounting measures of performance, such as financial ratios, indicate a relatively stable performance immediately prior to the crisis. Increasing risk—indicated by higher leverage, an increase in the proportion of distressed firms, and the lower proportion of long-term to total debt—meant, however, that risk-adjusted returns were deteriorating. Stock market returns in individual markets in the crisis countries declined as well in the run-up to the crisis. Measures of efficiency also indicate that corporate performance worsened in the precrisis period. The indicators point to some role for the decline to corporate-level fundamentals, such as performance and sustainability, in explaining the crisis, particularly in Korea and Thailand. More recently, the corporate sector in Malaysia has benefited from a strong economic recovery and lower interest rates, and the accounting measures of corporate performance show significant improvement in 1999, although measures of efficiency have not improved.

An assessment of corporate reforms shows that significant progress has been achieved with debt restructuring, and concerted efforts have been made toward improving corporate governance. There is, however, less evidence of operational restructuring over and above labor shedding, and efficiency measures—adjusting for changes in exogenous circumstances—suggest that the benefits of operational restructuring have not yet led to increases in firm efficiency.

While an analysis of corporate performance in Malaysia finds a number of possible links between the corporate sector and the crisis, the failure of corporate governance is an underlying theme. As in other Asian countries, the net worth of a firm—rather than the profit potential of a particular undertaking—is an important determinant of how much a firm can borrow in Malaysia. Such a mechanism is likely to lead to an inefficient allocation of funds and to the balance sheet problem, both of which may exacerbate the effects of a shock that reduces the wealth of a firm. Also, evidence indicates that corporations in Malaysia, and in the other Asian countries, were increasing leverage despite their declining profitability, referred to as the "Asia Bet" by Harvey and Roper (1999). Increasingly, corporations were tapping short-term and foreign debt markets, effectively betting that exchange rates would remain stable: they lost both bets. The close links between the corporate sector and the financial sector and the lack of a well-developed corporate bond market also led to overreliance on bank lending.

Thus, it could be argued that the system of corporate governance led to inefficient allocation of funds, created innate vulnerabilities in the corporate sector, and failed to discipline managers and contain the risks they assumed. The importance of good governance is clear, and to achieve it requires better monitoring of managers, improved information quality and availability, and transparency in corporate management. Adoption of the recommendations of the Finance Committee's Report on Corporate Governance is proceeding well and, if fully implemented and adhered to in spirit, will significantly enhance corporate governance in Malaysia. These reforms will take time to implement and become effective, but momentum should not be lost because of improving or deteriorating corporate and general economic performance.

There is significant evidence of a deterioration in corporate sector performance, but it does not appear to be commensurate with the resulting crisis. If the decline in corporate fundamentals did not justify the extent of the crisis in Malaysia, then the role of contagion, the balance sheet problem, and the transfer problem suggest the type of crisis described by the model in Krugman (1999). The implications for avoiding such crises are similar to those suggested above. A more specific implication is the reduction in the reliance on short-term debt and external debt—both are key to the feedback mechanism—to reduce susceptibility to sudden losses of confidence, resulting in self-fulfilling crises. Once such a crisis is under way, it is clear that sufficiently large funds from a lender-of-last-resort could restore confidence and avoid a downward spiral and protracted crisis. In reality, the amounts needed are very large and their availability may create moral hazard.

References

Bank Negara Malaysia, 1999, *Annual Report* (Kuala Lumpur).

Berg, Andrew, and others, 1999, *Anticipating Balance of Payments Crises: The Role of Early Warning Systems*, IMF Occasional Paper No. 186 (Washington: International Monetary Fund).

Bernake, Ben, and Marie Gertler, 1995, "Inside the Black Box: The Credit Channel of Monetary Policy Transmission," *Journal of Economic Perspectives*, Vol.9 (Fall), pp. 27–48.

Chang, Roberto, and Andrés Velasco, 1998, "Financial Crisis in Emerging Markets: A Canonical Model," NBER Working Paper No. 6606 (Cambridge, Massachusetts: National Bureau of Economic Research).

Claessens, Stijn, Simeon Djankov, and Larry Lang, 1998, "Who Controls East Asian Corporations?" IMF Seminar Series, No. 1999-6, pp. 1–40.

———, 1999, "Corporate Diversification in East Asia: The Role of Ultimate Ownership and Group Affiliation," Policy Research Working Papers No. 2089 (Washington: World Bank).

Claessens, Stijn, Simeon Djankov, and Daniela Klingebiel, 1999, "Bank and Corporate Restructuring in East Asia: Opportunities for Further Reform," paper presented at International Monetary Fund Annual Meetings seminar, Washington, September.

Claessens, Stijn, Simeon Djankov, and Lixine Xu, 2000, "Corporate Performance in the East Asian Financial Crisis," *The World Bank Research Observer*, Vol. 15, pp. 23–46.

Corsetti, Giancarlo, Paolo Pesenti, and Nouriel Roubini, 1998, "What Caused the Asian Currency and Financial Crisis? A Macroeconomic Overview," NBER Working Paper No. 6833 (Cambridge, Massachusetts: National Bureau of Economic Research).

Crama, Yves, and others, 1999, "Corporate Governance Structures, Control and Performance in European Markets: A Tale of Two Systems," Center for Economic Research Discussion Paper No. 9942 (Louvain, Belgium: Catholic University of Louvain).

Diamond, Douglas, and Philip Dybvig, 1983, "Bank Runs, Deposit Insurance, and Liquidity," *Journal of Political Economy*, Vol. 91 (June), pp. 401–19.

Dollar, David, and Mary Hallward-Driemeier, 2000, "Crisis, Adjustment, and Reform in Thailand's Industrial Firms," *The World Bank Research Observer*, Vol. 15 (Washington: World Bank), pp. 1–22.

Färe, Rolf, Shawna Grosskopf, and C.A. Knox Lovell, 1994, *Production Frontiers* (Cambridge: Cambridge University Press).

Färe Rolf, and others, 1997, "Biased Technical Change and the Malmquist Productivity Index," *Scandinavian Journal of Economics*, Vol. 99 (March), pp. 119–27.

Furman, Jason, and Joseph Stiglitz, 1998, "Economic Crises: Evidence and Insights from East Asia," *Brookings Papers on Economic Activity*, Vol. 2 (Washington: Brookings Institution), pp. 1–114.

Ghosh, Swati, and Atish Ghosh, 1999, "East Asia in the Aftermath: Was There a Crunch?" IMF Working Paper 99/38 (Washington: International Monetary Fund).

Harvey, C., and A. Roper, 1999, "The Asian Bet," in *Financial Markets and Development: The Crisis in Emerging Financial Markets*, Alison Harwood, Robert E. Litan, and Michael Pomerleano, eds. (Washington: Brookings Institution Press), pp. 29–115.

Johnson, Simon, and others, 1998, "Corporate Governance in the Asian Financial Crisis, 1997–98," MIT, mimeo (Cambridge, Massachusetts: Massachusetts Institute of Technology).

Kochhar, Kalpana, and others, 1999, *Malaysia—Selected Issues*, IMF Staff Country Report No. 99/86 (Washington: International Monetary Fund).

Krugman, Paul, 1992, "A Model of Balance-of-Payments Crises," *Currencies and Crises* (Cambridge: MIT Press), pp. 61–76.

———, 1998, "What Happened to Asia?" paper presented at a conference in Japan, January (Cambridge: MIT). Available via the Internet: *http://web.mit.edu/krugman/www/#other*.

———, 1999, "Balance Sheets, the Transfer Problem, and Financial Crises," paper prepared for the festschrift volume in honor of Robert Flood, MIT, Cambridge. Available via the Internet: *http://web.mit. edu/ krugman/www/#other*.

La Porta, Rafael, Florencio Lopez-de-Silanes, and Andrei Shleifer, 1998, "Corporate Ownership Around the World," NBER Working Paper No. 6625 (Cambridge, Massachusetts: National Bureau of Economic Research).

———, 1999, "Investor Protection: Origins, Consequences, Reform," NBER Working Paper No. 7428 (Cambridge, Massachusetts: National Bureau of Economic Research).

Malmquist, Sten, 1953, "Index Numbers and Indifference Surfaces," *Trabajos de Estadística*, Vol. 4, pp. 209–42.

Obstfeld, Maurice, 1986, "Rational and Self-Fulfilling Balance of Payments Crises," *American Economic Review*, Vol. 76 (March), pp. 72–81.

Pomerleano, Michael, 1998, "The East Asia Crisis and Corporate Finances: The Untold Micro Story," World Bank Policy Research Working Paper No. 1990 (Washington: World Bank).

Radelet, Steven, and Jeffrey Sachs, 1998, "The Onset of the East Asian Financial Crisis," NBER Working

Paper No. 6680 (Cambridge, Massachusetts: National Bureau of Economic Research).

Stiglitz, Joseph, and Andrew Weiss, 1981, "Credit Rationing in Markets with Imperfect Information," *American Economic Review*, Vol. 71, pp. 393–410.

World Bank, 1998, *East Asia: Road to Recovery* (Washington: World Bank).

———, 1999a, *East Asia: Recovery and Beyond* (Washington: World Bank).

———, 1999b, "Malaysia Structural Policy Review: Path to Recovery," Report No. 18647-MA, June (Washington: World Bank).

———, forthcoming, *Malaysia: Corporate Governance Assessment* (Washington: World Bank).

Recent Occasional Papers of the International Monetary Fund

207. Malaysia: From Crisis to Recovery, by Kanitta Meesook, Il Houng Lee, Olin Liu, Yougesh Khatri, Natalia Tamirisa, Michael Moore, and Mark H. Krysl. 2001.

206. The Dominican Republic: Stabilization, Structural Reform, and Economic Growth, by Alessandro Giustiniani, Werner C. Keller, and Randa E. Sab. 2001

205. Stabilization and Savings Funds for Nonrenewable Resources, by Jeffrey Davis, Rolando Ossowski, James Daniel, and Steven Barnett. 2001.

204. Monetary Union in West Africa (ECOWAS): Is It Desirable and How Could It Be Achieved? by Paul Masson and Catherine Pattillo. 2001.

203. Modern Banking and OTC Derivatives Markets: The Transformation of Global Finance and Its Implications for Systemic Risk, by Garry J. Schinasi, R. Sean Craig, Burkhard Drees, and Charles Kramer. 2000.

202. Adopting Inflation Targeting: Practical Issues for Emerging Market Countries, by Andrea Schaechter, Mark R. Stone, and Mark Zelmer. 2000.

201. Developments and Challenges in the Caribbean Region, by Samuel Itam, Simon Cueva, Erik Lundback, Janet Stotsky, and Stephen Tokarick. 2000.

200. Pension Reform in the Baltics: Issues and Prospects, by Jerald Schiff, Niko Hobdari, Axel Schimmelpfennig, and Roman Zytek. 2000.

199. Ghana: Economic Development in a Democratic Environment, by Sérgio Pereira Leite, Anthony Pellechio, Luisa Zanforlin, Girma Begashaw, Stefania Fabrizio, and Joachim Harnack. 2000.

198. Setting Up Treasuries in the Baltics, Russia, and Other Countries of the Former Soviet Union: An Assessment of IMF Technical Assistance, by Barry H. Potter and Jack Diamond. 2000.

197. Deposit Insurance: Actual and Good Practices, by Gillian G.H. Garcia. 2000.

196. Trade and Trade Policies in Eastern and Southern Africa, by a staff team led by Arvind Subramanian, with Enrique Gelbard, Richard Harmsen, Katrin Elborgh-Woytek, and Piroska Nagy. 2000.

195. The Eastern Caribbean Currency Union—Institutions, Performance, and Policy Issues, by Frits van Beek, José Roberto Rosales, Mayra Zermeño, Ruby Randall, and Jorge Shepherd. 2000.

194. Fiscal and Macroeconomic Impact of Privatization, by Jeffrey Davis, Rolando Ossowski, Thomas Richardson, and Steven Barnett. 2000.

193. Exchange Rate Regimes in an Increasingly Integrated World Economy, by Michael Mussa, Paul Masson, Alexander Swoboda, Esteban Jadresic, Paolo Mauro, and Andy Berg. 2000.

192. Macroprudential Indicators of Financial System Soundness, by a staff team led by Owen Evans, Alfredo M. Leone, Mahinder Gill, and Paul Hilbers. 2000.

191. Social Issues in IMF-Supported Programs, by Sanjeev Gupta, Louis Dicks-Mireaux, Ritha Khemani, Calvin McDonald, and Marijn Verhoeven. 2000.

190. Capital Controls: Country Experiences with Their Use and Liberalization, by Akira Ariyoshi, Karl Habermeier, Bernard Laurens, Inci Ötker-Robe, Jorge Iván Canales Kriljenko, and Andrei Kirilenko. 2000.

189. Current Account and External Sustainability in the Baltics, Russia, and Other Countries of the Former Soviet Union, by Donal McGettigan. 2000.

188. Financial Sector Crisis and Restructuring: Lessons from Asia, by Carl-Johan Lindgren, Tomás J.T. Baliño, Charles Enoch, Anne-Marie Gulde, Marc Quintyn, and Leslie Teo. 1999.

187. Philippines: Toward Sustainable and Rapid Growth, Recent Developments and the Agenda Ahead, by Markus Rodlauer, Prakash Loungani, Vivek Arora, Charalambos Christofides, Enrique G. De la Piedra, Piyabha Kongsamut, Kristina Kostial, Victoria Summers, and Athanasios Vamvakidis. 2000.

186. Anticipating Balance of Payments Crises: The Role of Early Warning Systems, by Andrew Berg, Eduardo Borensztein, Gian Maria Milesi-Ferretti, and Catherine Pattillo. 1999.

185. Oman Beyond the Oil Horizon: Policies Toward Sustainable Growth, edited by Ahsan Mansur and Volker Treichel. 1999.

184. Growth Experience in Transition Countries, 1990–98, by Oleh Havrylyshyn, Thomas Wolf, Julian Berengaut, Marta Castello-Branco, Ron van Rooden, and Valerie Mercer-Blackman. 1999.

183. Economic Reforms in Kazakhstan, Kyrgyz Republic, Tajikistan, Turkmenistan, and Uzbekistan, by Emine Gürgen, Harry Snoek, Jon Craig, Jimmy McHugh, Ivailo Izvorski, and Ron van Rooden. 1999.

182. Tax Reform in the Baltics, Russia, and Other Countries of the Former Soviet Union, by a staff team led by Liam Ebrill and Oleh Havrylyshyn. 1999.

181. The Netherlands: Transforming a Market Economy, by C. Maxwell Watson, Bas B. Bakker, Jan Kees Martijn, and Ioannis Halikias. 1999.

180. Revenue Implications of Trade Liberalization, by Liam Ebrill, Janet Stotsky, and Reint Gropp. 1999.

179. Disinflation in Transition: 1993–97, by Carlo Cottarelli and Peter Doyle. 1999.

178. IMF-Supported Programs in Indonesia, Korea, and Thailand: A Preliminary Assessment, by Timothy Lane, Atish Ghosh, Javier Hamann, Steven Phillips, Marianne Schulze-Ghattas, and Tsidi Tsikata. 1999.

177. Perspectives on Regional Unemployment in Europe, by Paolo Mauro, Eswar Prasad, and Antonio Spilimbergo. 1999.

176. Back to the Future: Postwar Reconstruction and Stabilization in Lebanon, edited by Sena Eken and Thomas Helbling. 1999.

175. Macroeconomic Developments in the Baltics, Russia, and Other Countries of the Former Soviet Union, 1992–97, by Luis M. Valdivieso. 1998.

174. Impact of EMU on Selected Non–European Union Countries, by R. Feldman, K. Nashashibi, R. Nord, P. Allum, D. Desruelle, K. Enders, R. Kahn, and H. Temprano-Arroyo. 1998.

173. The Baltic Countries: From Economic Stabilization to EU Accession, by Julian Berengaut, Augusto Lopez-Claros, Françoise Le Gall, Dennis Jones, Richard Stern, Ann-Margret Westin, Effie Psalida, Pietro Garibaldi. 1998.

172. Capital Account Liberalization: Theoretical and Practical Aspects, by a staff team led by Barry Eichengreen and Michael Mussa, with Giovanni Dell'Ariccia, Enrica Detragiache, Gian Maria Milesi-Ferretti, and Andrew Tweedie. 1998.

171. Monetary Policy in Dollarized Economies, by Tomás Baliño, Adam Bennett, and Eduardo Borensztein. 1998.

170. The West African Economic and Monetary Union: Recent Developments and Policy Issues, by a staff team led by Ernesto Hernández-Catá and comprising Christian A. François, Paul Masson, Pascal Bouvier, Patrick Peroz, Dominique Desruelle, and Athanasios Vamvakidis. 1998.

169. Financial Sector Development in Sub-Saharan African Countries, by Hassanali Mehran, Piero Ugolini, Jean Phillipe Briffaux, George Iden, Tonny Lybek, Stephen Swaray, and Peter Hayward. 1998.

168. Exit Strategies: Policy Options for Countries Seeking Greater Exchange Rate Flexibility, by a staff team led by Barry Eichengreen and Paul Masson with Hugh Bredenkamp, Barry Johnston, Javier Hamann, Esteban Jadresic, and Inci Ötker. 1998.

167. Exchange Rate Assessment: Extensions of the Macroeconomic Balance Approach, edited by Peter Isard and Hamid Faruqee. 1998

166. Hedge Funds and Financial Market Dynamics, by a staff team led by Barry Eichengreen and Donald Mathieson with Bankim Chadha, Anne Jansen, Laura Kodres, and Sunil Sharma. 1998.

165. Algeria: Stabilization and Transition to the Market, by Karim Nashashibi, Patricia Alonso-Gamo, Stefania Bazzoni, Alain Féler, Nicole Laframboise, and Sebastian Paris Horvitz. 1998.

164. MULTIMOD Mark III: The Core Dynamic and Steady-State Model, by Douglas Laxton, Peter Isard, Hamid Faruqee, Eswar Prasad, and Bart Turtelboom. 1998.

163. Egypt: Beyond Stabilization, Toward a Dynamic Market Economy, by a staff team led by Howard Handy. 1998.

Note: For information on the title and availability of Occasional Papers not listed, please consult the IMF Publications Catalog or contact IMF Publication Services.